On the Road with Ruth

Faith for the Journey

Andrea Lennon

True Vine Ministry
Conway, Arkansas

Printed by CreateSpace,
a division of Amazon Publishing

ISBN-13:978-1508874560
ISBN-10:1508874565

Printed in the United States of America

Cover art by Sam Raynor of Grace Shall Reign
Author photo by Becky Mathis of Rear Window Collection

Additional copies of this book can be ordered at
www.andrealennon.net or www.amazon.com

Contents

Introduction   7

Chapter 1: Clinging to the Right Things   11

Chapter 2: Living with Determination   25

Chapter 3: Engaging in Life   38

Chapter 4: Finding a Safe Place   50

Chapter 5: Being a Life-Giver   60

Chapter 6: Waiting and Watching   74

Chapter 7: Blessed to Be a Blessing   85

Epilogue   97

About the Author   99
   Free to Thrive
   Reflecting His Glory

Bibliography   103

DEDICATION

I dedicate this book to the loving memory of Madelyn Grace Johnston. Madelyn's family and friends remember her as a young girl who loved Jesus, was full of personality, saw the best in others, and embraced life each day. Madelyn died at the young age of eight. Family and friends gathered the night of the accident and began the long process of grieving. In that pain-filled moment, as several of us sat in her room, I looked up at her wall. Scripture verses that Madelyn had been memorizing were written on cards and hanging there; Psalm 23 was next to Madelyn's bed. Without a doubt, the Lord was (and is) Madelyn's Shepherd.

A few days after Madelyn's death, a treasure was found. It was a handwritten prayer that Madelyn wrote to God about her Second Baptist Church family. Amazingly, at eight years old, Madelyn understood that God gave her everything she needed.

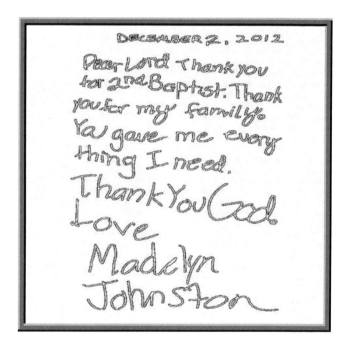

My last memory of Madelyn is of her dancing and doing cartwheels in the fellowship hall of our church just days before her death. Each time I think of Madelyn, I think of her dancing and doing cartwheels. The only difference – now she is doing them for Jesus. I say with all my heart, "Dance, sweet Madelyn, dance and do cartwheels for Jesus."

Introduction

The journey begins....

The story of Ruth provides a powerful reminder that God calls people from unlikely backgrounds and ordinary beginnings to take part in His amazing plan. Ruth, one of the central characters in the story, was a Moabite woman. In today's culture it may seem insignificant that Ruth was from Moab or that she was a woman. The more we study the story and its setting, though, the more we see how shockingly counter-cultural it was! Women in Ruth's day were viewed as property. Their thoughts, feelings, and preferences were rarely, if ever, taken into consideration. In the working class, women were expected to help with farming as well as bear children and take care of the family. Even in the God-fearing Israelite culture, they had little say in marriage or life direction. In neighboring countries, such as Moab, prostitution and idolatry were common and brought their own dangers and temptations. *The fact that God included a Moabite woman in His plan of redemption speaks volumes about the way God values everyone no matter their age, gender, background, race, or social standing.* Throughout history, we see that God has enjoyed using unlikely people to display His amazing grace.

Our approach to studying Ruth's story will be simple. As we go through the chapters, we will stop each time we encounter a character quality in Ruth's life that honored the Lord. This approach will allow us to put ourselves in Ruth's position and feel the weight of her circumstances. We will then ask ourselves an important question, "How does the lesson we learn here apply to our own lives?" In this book we will focus on *having the right set of beliefs, on displaying Christ-like character in our daily life, and on embracing an eternal perspective*. All of this will help us grow more confident in our faith journey.

In order to get the most out of this book, we need to do two things. First, we need to read the book of Ruth, as recorded in the Bible, several times. (I suggest reading the book of Ruth prior to reading each chapter in this book). Ruth is made up of four short chapters, and it reads like a novel, which makes it easy to get into. We'll walk with Ruth through crossroads, into a town full of strangers, and into harvest fields as God's plan for her life unfolds. To me, the most intriguing part of Ruth's story was her willingness to trust God through all the changes. At some point in Ruth's life, she came to find her identity in her relationship with the One True God. As a result, Ruth willingly gave up everything that she knew—her homeland, her family, her friends, and her old gods.

Second, we need to understand the layout of each chapter in this book. Each chapter begins with the **Her Journey** section. This is the part of the chapter that provides the story line of the main characters as recorded in the Bible. In the **Her Journey** section, we will learn interesting facts about life in Moab and Bethlehem. The main characters will become like friends as we read about life in their day as well as the challenges they faced. Following the **Her Journey** section, the character quality is introduced. The character quality relates to the beliefs, actions, and perspectives that we see in the lives of the main characters. As we examine the character quality, we'll go over additional Scripture passages. These passages will help us to understand the significance of the character quality in our walk with God. Finally, there is the **Our Journey** section. This shows us how the character quality can be applied to our daily walk with Jesus. There are also application questions so that book clubs, Bible study groups, and individual readers can discuss the main points of the chapter.

I hope you are ready for an adventure—we have a fascinating journey ahead! Let's begin with prayer.

Heavenly Father,

It is with humble hearts that we begin this journey. How exciting to know that You, the God of the universe, created us to know, love, and serve You! As we start this book, we know that You have a meaningful message for us. Lord, we want to learn from You. Thank You for the life of Ruth; thank You for using an unlikely person to accomplish Your perfect plan. Lord, we are here and we are also unlikely. Equip us with Your truth so that we can discern the right steps to take. Use this book to challenge us to live in a way that daily demonstrates Your power as we walk in step with You.

In the loving and powerful name of Jesus we pray...amen and amen.

Chapter 1
Clinging to the Right Things

I am excited to share this adventure through the story of Ruth with you. This story deals with heartbreak, loss, and pain. It also deals with healing, hope, and the ultimate restoration that comes from God through Jesus Christ. While I do not know the details of your life, I know that God has led you to this resource for a reason. *No matter what you're facing, God is at work in your life.*

Before you begin, may I ask you to do one thing? Please take a moment and read the introduction to this book. The introduction sets the stage for Ruth's story. I promise you do not want to miss this important background information. Once you have read the introduction, begin this book with an open heart, expecting God to speak to you. It excites me to know that God can use His Word to teach us new lessons, no matter how familiar we may be with a story like Ruth's.

Her Journey

The book of Ruth opens with a family of four fleeing their homeland in search of food. The opening verses provide important details that help the reader to understand the setting of the story, the heritage of four of the main characters, and the challenges they faced.

"In the days when the judges ruled, there was a famine in the land. So a man from Bethlehem in Judah, together with his wife and two sons, went to live for a while in the country of Moab. The man's name was Elimelek, his wife's name was Naomi, and the names of his two sons were Mahlon and Kilion. They were Ephrathites from Bethlehem, Judah. And they went to Moab and lived there." (Ruth 1:1-2)

Have you ever been truly hungry? Hungry to the point where you did something that you never dreamed possible? As refugees from the famine, Elimelek and his family trekked off to an infamous neighboring country, leaving behind their home in the promised land of Canaan. The promised land was known as a place of physical rest and physical abundance, a prime piece of land flowing with milk and honey. God promised this land to Abram, (later known as Abraham) and his descendants in Genesis 12. In Genesis 15, God entered into a covenant with Abram ensuring that his descendants would inherit the land. That is exactly what happened.

Abraham's descendants eventually migrated to Egypt, and later those descendants, known as Israelites, were enslaved by the Egyptians. God delivered His people from Egyptian slavery through a man named Moses, who was also descended from Abraham. Moses led the Israelites to the edge of the promised land of Canaan, but there they failed to obey God's instructions for entering it and were forced back. After 40 years of wandering in the desert, the Israelites entered the promised land and began the long process of possessing it. Canaan was a dream come true for God's people who had been enslaved and never had a place to call their own. The produce that grew in the land was massive. Scripture speaks of two men carrying a single cluster of grapes using a long wooden pole that rested on each man's shoulder. Without a doubt, God provided an amazing place for His people to live.

With God's provision came clear instruction. God's people were to take full possession of the land and drive out all the inhabitants. Unfortunately, the Israelites failed to obey. Instead, they allowed the inhabitants to influence them to join in customs of immorality and idolatry. A cycle of sin became the norm for the Israelites.

The cycle of sin was predictable. The people sinned. God sent consequences. The people cried out to God for help. God sent a judge to rescue the people and reestablish godly principles. The people prospered only to fall back into the painful trap of sin. Sound familiar? Just think how often we follow a similar pattern in our lives.

It was during one of these cycles of sin that God sent a famine to the land of Judah. This famine ravaged the towns of Judah, such as Bethlehem. God sent this famine to get His people's attention, reminding them that sin is serious and always carries a consequence. It is interesting to note that the name Bethlehem means "house of bread." The implication of this name is ironic; there was no bread in the "house of bread."

The heart attitude of the Israelites during the time of Elimelek is best summed up in Judges 21:25, "In those days there was no king in Israel; everyone did as they saw fit." We see this happening vividly as Elimelek and Naomi left Bethlehem in search of food, migrating to the unlikely country of Moab.

The Moabite people traced their beginnings to an incident of incest by Abraham's nephew Lot with his own daughter. (Genesis 19:30-37) The atmosphere of Moab during Elimelek's day was equally perverse. There was no respect for the One True God. The chief god of the Moabite people was Chemosh; worship of Chemosh and other gods included child sacrifice and sexual promiscuity. This was the atmosphere that Elimelek and his family faced as they settled into life in their new home.

Once in Moab, Elimelek's family experienced a series of tragic events. First, Elimelek died. We do not know what happened to Elimelek. What we do know is that Naomi was left with her two sons. Interestingly, the meanings behind the names weren't optimistic. Mahlon meant "sickly," while Kilion meant "weakly."

While in Moab, the sons met and married Moabite women. Scripture is quiet on how the couples met and the way they lived. Only a few important details are included. The names of the Moabite women were Ruth and Orpah. Scripture tells us that neither Ruth nor Orpah was able to bear children. This reality must have been difficult for everyone to accept, since family survival often depended on child bearing. After ten years of marriage, both men died.

Following the deaths of Elimelek, Mahlon, and Kilion, Naomi was left with a broken heart and two widowed Moabite daughters-in-law. When Naomi arrived in Moab her life was hard, but at least she had a husband and two sons. Several years later, she must have wondered why these tragedies happened. Why had God forsaken her?

One day, word reached Moab that the Lord had come to the aid of His people in Bethlehem by providing food. This news forced Naomi to make an important decision. Would she stay in Moab, or would she return to Bethlehem?

Naomi chose to return to her homeland. I wonder how many sleepless nights she had as she prepared for the long journey home, pondering an unsure future. What would life be like in Bethlehem? Would she be accepted or rejected? How would she explain the loss her family experienced in Moab? What would people think?

Ruth and Orpah accompanied her for the first part of the journey. Then Naomi pleaded with her daughters-in-law to return to their families in Moab. "'Go back, each of you, to your mother's home. May the Lord show you kindness, as you have shown kindness to your dead husbands and to me. May the Lord grant that each of you will find rest in the home of another husband.' Then she kissed them goodbye and they wept aloud." (Ruth 1:8-9)

An important word is introduced to us here in Naomi's plea to Ruth and Orpah. The word is the Hebrew *hesed*, translated as "kindness" in verse 8. Naomi was familiar with the concept of *hesed* because of her Jewish roots. It represented one of the most important concepts in the Old Testament; God used this word to describe His own character. *Hesed* can be translated as "kindness" or "love." It also meant mercy and faithfulness, especially to one less fortunate.[i] When Naomi used the word *hesed*, she gave us a peek into a special type of relationship, one characterized by loyalty.

When Naomi encouraged Ruth and Orpah to return to Moab, she could have done so for at least two reasons. Maybe Naomi did not want her daughters-in-law to experience the difficult days that lay ahead in Bethlehem. Maybe Naomi was worried about the hardship it would create for her if she brought two Moabite women home, since Israelites were instructed to never marry foreigners. Either way, we can hear and feel the emotion in Naomi's plea, "Turn back! Turn back! Turn back!"

According to Scripture, Orpah struggled with her decision. Should she continue on the journey to Bethlehem or should she go back? After many tears, Orpah returned to Moab. We have no biblical evidence to answer some of our pressing questions. Did Orpah make it back home? Did Orpah remarry? Did she have children? Did she place her faith in the One True God? Scripture remains silent on the rest of Orpah's story, but, thankfully, not about Ruth's.

Ruth stood on the road and considered two different lives: a life that had been in Moab and a life that could be in Israel. She refused to turn back. "Orpah kissed her mother-in-law goodbye, but Ruth clung to her." (Ruth 1:14) The word *clung* that is used in this passage is a strong one. In fact, it is the same word that is used in Genesis 2:24 to describe the bond created by marriage.

Ruth's feelings are summed up in Ruth 1:16-18: "Don't urge me

14

to leave you or to turn back from you. Where you go I will go, and where you stay I will stay. Your people will be my people and your God my God. Where you die I will die, and there I will be buried. May the Lord deal with me, be it ever so severely, if anything but death separates you and me."

What a powerful proclamation of love! Ruth no longer considered the Moabite people to be her people. Her people would be God's chosen people the Israelites. When Ruth became the wife of Naomi's son, her life was forever changed. Her allegiance had moved from one culture to another culture, and, even more importantly, to the One True God. Through it all, God was positioning Ruth to live in a way that she never dreamed possible.

Clinging to the right things in life

Clinging is important because it shows the real affections of our hearts. We cling to the things that we love and value. We cling to the things that matter the most to us. Ultimately, clinging impacts the way we walk on this earth. Clinging determines if we live for Jesus or if we live for ourselves.

Godly clinging begins deep in our hearts and minds. Fueled by our belief system, clinging determines the people, places, and actions that give direction to our lives. Godly clinging is shown each time that we hold tightly to biblical truth. This helps us to hold tenaciously to the right beliefs so that we can display the right actions in our daily walk with God.

While godly clinging is an action that requires active participation, godly clinging is also a resolve. We exhibit this resolve each time we choose to embrace the journey God has for us, no matter how hard, surprising, or wonderful it turns out. Think of how easy it is to run from God. Sometimes we run from God because we think, "I'm not good enough." "This life is too hard." "I did not know I was signing up for this...."

We do not know when Ruth placed her trust in the One True God, clinging to God and His plan for her life. What we do know is that when Ruth clung to Naomi, she chose a new direction for her life. She made the decision to leave the past in the past. As she walked away from Moab, Ruth said good-bye to everything that was familiar, predictable, and comfortable. As she did, Ruth embraced a future that was vastly different than anything she could have imagined.

Our beliefs about God are important. Our beliefs provide the basis of truth that we use to build our lives upon. Let's examine three important beliefs about God that help us cling to Him.

God is the ultimate authority over our lives. Have you heard the statement that God is sovereign? Although we do not use the word *sovereign* very often, it is a great word to describe God. God's sovereignty teaches us that He has power and that He is in charge of the people and the things that He has created. Nothing exists outside of God's wisdom, knowledge, power, and care. Our lives are not an accident. We serve the One True God who created us and willingly directs our steps. As God directs our steps, He positions us to fulfill His purposes for our lives. Psalm 24:1 speaks about the fact that God is in charge. "The earth is the Lord's, and everything in it, the world, and all who live in it." Psalm 103:19 also states, "The Lord has established his throne in heaven, and his kingdom rules over all."

God's sovereignty is connected to His holiness. The holiness of God is important for us to understand. It means that God is set apart, and God is spiritually pure. To be set apart means to be different. God is different from anyone or anything that He has created. There has never been a time when God did not exist or when He was not fully in charge. God is God. He has always been God, and He always will be God. To be spiritually pure means to be perfect. God has no sin within Him, not even a hint. He is the ultimate standard of perfection. As a result, we can know that God is good and that His work in our lives is good.

The sovereignty of God is important for us to understand and accept. Because of God's sovereignty, He has authority over our lives. How should we respond to this? We should praise Him and rely on Him for power and strength! Sometimes it is hard to praise God and rely on Him, but those are some of the most crucial moments for us to remember that God is in charge. Sometimes this means saying out loud, "God, I know that you are in control and that nothing about my life surprises you!"

God's sovereignty is beyond our human ability to fully understand. The human mind cannot grasp the greatness of our God. The sovereignty of God does not mean we have to give up our free will, our God-given right to make choices. God loves us, and He wants us to love Him and to respond to Him in faith. Since both the sovereignty of God and the free will of man are taught in the Bible, believers do not have to choose one teaching over the other— we can fully embrace both. Since we do not understand fully how they work together, the combination stays a beautiful mystery. God is in charge, and we also have the opportunity to respond to Him in faith.

God is directing the events of our lives. Each moment of each day God guides, sustains, cares, loves, and longs to have fellowship with us. God is always at work in us and around us. God is purposeful in the way that He works. We can trust the heart and hand of God. Not only is God leading us, He is also preparing the way so that we can experience victory in our daily walks with Him. *Without exception, God knows what is best for us in every situation that we face.*

The truth that God is directing the events of our lives does not prevent times of difficulty or pain; believers are not guaranteed a problem-free life. When sin entered this world, bad things like death, disease, and difficulty became a reality that every person would face. However, we should not be discouraged. God is ultimately in control, and His presence is always with us. We serve the One True God who is able to meet and exceed every need that we face in life. God promises to work all things (the easy things and the hard things) together for our good and for His glory. "And we know that in all things God works for the good of those who love him, who have been called according to his purpose." (Romans 8:28)

How should we respond to the truth that God is directing the events of our lives? We should trust Him! This type of trust comes from knowing that God is with us and that He is for us. We can know that we are placing our confidence in God when His peace permeates our hearts and minds.

Let's think about our hearts. God's peace enables us to have a quiet spirit instead of a "tizzy" type of spirit. A quiet spirit is a calm spirit. A calm spirit is filled with a peace that we cannot explain. This calmness is real, and it is apparent especially when we are in the middle of an unknown or uncomfortable situation yet have an unexplainable peace. A "tizzy" type of spirit is much different. It brings a feeling of being out of control, as though life is one big roller coaster ride. The events of our day determine our moods. In a matter of minutes, we can go from extremes of happiness to despair, with no

17

peace to hold on to.

Let's think about our minds. A Spirit-led mind knows and finds peace in the fact that we do not have to solve our problems. This means that we do not have to rely on our own strengths, resources, or abilities to get through our day. Instead, we can rely on God's strengths, resources, and abilities to guide us. It is reassuring to know that we do not have to figure out how to overcome the messy situations of life. We can go to the Lord and know that He cares for us and willingly guides us each step of the way.

God is fulfilling a plan in and through our lives. It boggles my mind to think about the truth that God has a specific purpose for every member of creation—including me and you!

God's plan is fulfilled in two forms. First, in a general sense, God has a plan that is exactly the same for every believer in Jesus Christ. Romans 8:29 talks about God's general plan. "For those God foreknew he also predestined to be *conformed to the image of his Son.*" (italics added) This verse points out an important truth: it is God's plan for every believer in Jesus Christ to grow in his or her faith journey. Scripture refers to this as being conformed to the image of Christ. Conformity to Jesus Christ occurs when we exhibit Christ-like qualities in our lives, such as when we think, act, and react in ways that point others to Jesus. Each day we have the opportunity to wake up and serve God. As we do, we encounter situations and circumstances that God uses to change us into the person He is calling us to be.

Here is one example. Suppose yesterday you had a short temper with a coworker and said something that was hurtful instead of helpful. Last night you prayed about it, and at work today, you were able to have a more patient attitude with her. A specific outcome of God's general plan for our lives is that *when we go to bed at night we are more like Jesus in the way that we think, act, and react, than when we woke up that morning.* Why? Because during the day we were conformed to the image of Jesus.

Second, God has a specific plan that is unique, individual, and personal for every believer in Jesus. Ephesians 2:10 talks about this. "For we are God's handiwork, created in Christ Jesus to do good works, which God prepared in advance for us to do." Knowing that God has a specific plan for our lives gives us purpose and direction Whether it is leading a Bible study, caring for a foster child, taking meal to someone in need, going on a mission trip, or singing on a praise team, God's specific plan invites us to step out of our comfort zone and live a life of faith. When we live a life of faith, we focus on God and His ability to work in and through us. This focus helps us to move beyond the difficulty of the past, the confusion of the present, and the looming fears of the future.

How should we respond to the plan of God? We should surrender to God's will by obeying. (So simple, yet so hard!) God desires hearts that say, "Yes, Lord," even before we know the request. He wants our simple obedience. He wants us to be ready to say, "Lord, wherever you tell me to go, I will go. Lord, whatever you tell me to do, I will do." No excuses. No second-guessing. No loopholes. Simple obedience even when life is hard or does not make sense. Simple obedience even when we do not feel qualified to answer the call. Simple obedience even when the surrounding people discourage us.

Our Journey

Ruth's life offers a perfect example of how God is the ultimate authority, how He is directing the events of our lives, and how He is fulfilling a plan. God lovingly created Ruth. God faithfully directed Ruth's steps. God purposefully had a plan for Ruth's life to fulfill. She chose to respond with obedience.

Just like Ruth, we have the opportunity to cling to God and His plan for our lives. For just a moment, place yourself in Ruth's position. You are facing a life-altering decision, a crossroads in your life. Will you move ahead or will you turn back? Will you cling to the "life that had been" or will you pursue the "life that could be?" Ultimately, your decision is determined by your foundational beliefs about who God is and what He is doing in your life. If you trust God and believe His Word, you will cling to Him in every area of life, even to the point of letting go of comfortable living.

Clinging to godly things means interacting with the right people, in the right places, and demonstrating the right daily actions. Let's think about how the right people, places, and actions impact our daily walk with God.

The Right People

When Ruth chose to cling to Naomi and to Naomi's people, she opened the door to relationships that would help her cling to God. While we may not be called to move somewhere new, it is crucial for us to find and cling to the right people. These people may come in expected forms like close family members, supportive church friends, or encouraging co-workers. Or, these people may come in unexpected forms like new acquaintances, online blog friends, or individuals of a different age or culture.

Filling our lives with the right people helps us to cling to godly living and positions us to move forward in our walk with God. How do you know who the right people are in your life? One test is answering this question. "When I am around _____, I am encouraged to love God and follow His plan for my life. When I am with _____, I make choices that please God and are in line with the Bible. True or false?" It is essential to be able to answer "True" to this statement about the people you regularly spend time with and who influence you the most.

One part of embracing the right people is learning how to let go of the wrong people. Certainly, Ruth knew about letting go. In order to embrace the Jewish people, she had to let go of the Moabite people. She could not cling to both. Remember Ruth's words to Naomi, "Your people will be my people." Ruth let go of the Moabite people so that her heart would be undivided. One division that many of us are familiar with is the need to please too many people. We act one way with one group and a different way with another group, and our lives becomes fragmented as we try to please all the people around us.

The people that we need to release are the people who distract us from our walk with God. These are the people who make excuses for us when we compromise. These are the people who encourage us to build a life that is more about money, success, or appearance and less about our eternal home. How do you know who the wrong people are in your life? One test is answering this question. "When I am around _____, I am encouraged to follow my own plan for my life, not God's plan. When I am with _____, I focus on what makes me happy or satisfies my immediate desire. True or false?" If you answer "True" to this question, it would be a good idea to pray about whether you should release this relationship.

It is important to note that releasing should not be done in a self-righteous or mean-spirited way. Releasing is nothing more than redefining a relationship. Often relationships have to be redefined so that our walk with God is not compromised. We can redefine the relationship by deciding where we will go and what we will do with the person. By choosing to set the tone for our interactions, we encourage situations that honor the Lord and are helpful in our walk with Him. *Be aware that the "right people" can include nonbelievers; the "wrong people" can include believers.* God places people in our life for many different reasons. This is why it is important to evaluate relationships individually.

- Who are the "right people" God has placed in your life?
- How do the "right people" help you to cling to God and His Word?
- Who are the "wrong people" that you need to release by redefining the relationship?
- What steps do you need to take in order to redefine this relationship in a Christ-honoring way?

The Right Places

God directs the events of our lives. We can know that God was in control in our past settings, He calls us to be faithful and wise in our present settings, and He will continue to direct us in our future settings. Our settings are important because they position us to fulfill God's plan for our lives. These settings include our schools, our churches, our jobs, and our social environments. These settings extend to the places where we grew up, the places where we currently live, and the places where we will live in the future.

Ruth grew up in Moab. She was a "hometown girl" who knew the Moabite culture. She probably knew people who sacrificed children to the gods and were caught up in promiscuity. We don't know the details of her life before she met Naomi's family, but I imagine her past had left her with some scars. We do know that Ruth still had a family in Moab, since Naomi encouraged Ruth to return to her mother's house.

For a season of Ruth's life, Moab was exactly where she needed to be. Although the dark environment grieved God, it served an important purpose. When it came time for Ruth to go to Bethlehem and join God's chosen people, the differences between Moab and Bethlehem would speak volumes about the character of God. There came a point in Ruth's life where she had to long for something more than Moab. She had to believe that there was a chance for a life that was full of hope and peace. She had to know that her life could be lovingly directed by the One True God.

Recently, I was sitting in a room full of women who serve as pastors' wives. Each lady shared her story of how she came to faith in Jesus Christ. Most of the stories began with, "At the age of six, Jesus saved me." Or, "I grew up in church, and I can't remember a time when I did not know that God loved me." I will never forget how one lady's testimony surprised us. She told us that she grew up in a family where God was not acknowledged. She told us about the patterns of hurt and sin through the first thirty or so years of her life. Then she shared how shocking it was to her when she encountered the love of Jesus Christ and the forgiveness that He offered her. "Every day I am thankful for my salvation. It makes a huge difference in my life," she finished. When I read Ruth's story, I wonder if she felt the same way. I wonder how she would have described the grace of God and the family of God, compared to what she had experienced in Moab.

- Do you have a "Moab" in your background? This could be a childhood full of abuse, or teenage years of neglect, or a draining relationship as an adult. Know that God sees you and longs to do a healing work in your life. Take heart in knowing that your past does not have to define or enslave you.
- If you're not sure you're in the right place, take inventory of your current settings. Are you living in a Moab? This question challenges you to examine your town, school, church, job, and social environments. (If you're living in an unsafe place, physically OR emotionally, reach out to someone in your church or a trusted friend who can help you with the next step in your journey).
- Think about your future settings. Do you feel God is leading you to a place that you are currently unwilling to go? If so, why? What is holding you back from embracing God's direction in your life?

The Right Actions

For just a moment allow this truth to sink in: God has a plan for you. God's plan is safe and secure in His heart and mind. God's plan for you is not out of His reach, nor is it out of His control. Rather,

God's plan is deliberate, and He provides everything that you need to fulfill His plan.

There are two ways to view God's specific plan for our lives. One way is by viewing His plan as fulfilled. An example can be found in verses like Psalm 139:16. "All the days ordained for me were written in your book before one of them came to be." Knowing that God has a plan and that God is able to bring His plan to pass provides great hope and confidence in following hard after Him.

The second way is to view God's plan as unfulfilled and as requiring our wholehearted obedience. This means that our actions are vitally important. (Check out Leviticus 26 and Deuteronomy 11)

Every day we make choices about where to go, what to do, and what to cling to. It is important to understand that we each have the ability to make choices that lead us to live inside or outside of God's plan for our lives. Choices that go against God's plan lead to heartache, a lack of peace, and a compromised ability to hear and respond to God's voice. In contrast, choices that please God position us to experience His best as we sense the blessing of God in every area of life. These blessings come in the form of God's peace, joy, power, presence, and confidence about the choices that we make.

The story of Ruth demonstrates how God's plan was fulfilled in her life. God had a specific plan for Ruth. God chose her, a foreigner, to be included in the lineage of Christ. This call on Ruth's life was vitally important to God's unfolding story of redemption. God demonstrated through Ruth's life that His grace is for all who believe. In Ruth's life we see the fulfillment of God's heart. He brings people who are deemed "not a people" to be His people (1 Peter 2:9).

God's plan for Ruth was sealed in His heart and mind before Ruth was born. Ruth did not have to earn God's call; she simply had to obey it. How did Ruth obey? She chose to follow God in the way that she lived her life. She made the choice to cling to Naomi no matter what. Even though Ruth had every right to turn back to Moab, she did not. Even though turning back to Moab would have made sense, she pressed on toward a new and different future—a future with God and His chosen people in Bethlehem.

Our daily actions matter. The places we go, the things we do, and the people we cling to need to be examined. The choices we make affect more than just us; they affect the people around us. As Ruth's story unfolds, we will see how her choice at that crossroads affected people in her day and continues to affect people in our day.

- Do you believe that God has a plan for your life?
- How is your level of confidence in God impacted by the truth that God's plan is secure in His heart and mind?
- In what areas of life do you need to demonstrate simple obedience? Is God calling you to go somewhere or do something specific? If so, what is holding you back from saying, "Lord, whatever you tell me to do, I will do"?
- Write down or share with a friend what you believe God's plan is for your life. If you are not sure, begin to pray about this matter. Ask a friend to pray with you.

Conclusion

Clinging to truth positions us to cling to the right people, places, and actions. This takes commitment, though. Clinging to the right things in life often goes against everything that feels normal or comfortable. As a result, when we cling to God and His plan for our lives, we may experience feelings of fear, anxiety, or loss of control; however, as we consistently cling to God and His Word, we will find that everything changes. These changes include our values, goals, and definitions of success. Slowly we will find that clinging to the right things brings a sense of peace and purpose. Ruth clung to Naomi. As she did, Ruth embraced the life God was calling her to. This led to truth being proclaimed in and through Ruth's life. By choosing to cling to the right things, she took one giant step forward in her walk with God. My question for you is this: Are you ready to do the same?

Chapter 2
Living With Determination

Her Journey

Standing on the road between Moab and Bethlehem, Naomi predicted a life of widowhood and poverty ahead. There would be no husbands, no children, and no hope. In Naomi's eyes, God's hand was against her. Her life was destined for bitterness. The weight of the situation is summed up in Naomi's plea for Ruth and Orpah to return to Moab. "Even if I thought there was still hope for me—even if I had a husband tonight and then gave birth to sons—would you wait until they grew up? Would you remain unmarried for them? No, my daughters. It is more bitter for me than for you, because the Lord's hand has turned against me!" (Ruth 1:12-13)

What Naomi said packed a powerful punch. Many words were spoken and many tears were shed. In the end, two decisions were made. Orpah returned to Moab. Ruth continued her journey to Bethlehem.

I try to put myself in each woman's position. Certainly the conversation was full of emotion. I have no doubt that Naomi loved her daughters-in-law. Scripture indicates that Naomi recognized the faithfulness of Ruth and Orpah. Naomi wanted Ruth and Orpah to have a good life. She wanted each of them to be loved and provided for by another husband. The only hope for this type of life, according to Naomi, was in Moab.

With a final embrace, Orpah walked out of Naomi's life. The last interaction between Naomi and Orpah was Naomi applauding Orpah's decision to return to Moab. Naomi tried to use Orpah's decision as an encouragement for Ruth to do the same. Ruth was not persuaded. In fact, Naomi could not find strong enough words to dissuade Ruth from returning to Bethlehem. "When Naomi realized that Ruth was determined to go with her, she stopped urging her." (Ruth 1:18)

It is impossible to know the exact location where the conversation between Naomi, Ruth, and Orpah took place. Some scholars believe that it was just a few miles outside of Moab. If that is the case, Naomi and Ruth had a long journey ahead of them. The distance between Moab and Bethlehem was around fifty miles, depending on the route taken. The trip was long, and it was not easy. The terrain was rugged and steep, requiring an uphill climb. It is believed that the trip took between seven to ten days to complete. Can you imagine how hard the trip was on Naomi and Ruth?

I have often thought about the conversations that took place between Naomi and Ruth as they journeyed. Based on Scripture, we can conclude that Naomi stopped urging Ruth to change her mind. As a result, I believe the conversation made an important transition– from looking back, to looking forward, from returning to Moab to surviving in Bethlehem. For Ruth, it would have been a crash course in all things Jewish. I wonder if this was the first time that Ruth realized how different life in Bethlehem would be from life in Moab.

We must consider Naomi's spiritual, emotional, and mental state if we want to fully understand what Ruth faced as she traveled to Bethlehem. Naomi admitted that she had no hope. She had lost her entire family. Naomi was focused on her pain, and it clouded her sight. She could not see her life from a place of healing or restoration. She could only see her life from a place of despair.

In her heart, did Ruth question Naomi's mindset? Did she think, "Is there maybe, just maybe, a good life waiting for us in Bethlehem?" Or, did Ruth assume that a life of widowhood and poverty was all she would know? Scripture is quiet on this subject. All we know is that Ruth had time to think about her life in Bethlehem as she and Naomi made the long journey.

Once in Bethlehem, word of Naomi's return created a great deal of excitement. The Bible tells us that everyone took note. The women exclaimed, "Can this be Naomi?" (Ruth 1:19) We should not be surprised at Naomi's response. "Don't call me Naomi," she told them. "Call me Mara, because the Almighty has made my life very bitter. I went away full, but the Lord has brought me back empty. Why call me Naomi? The Lord has afflicted me; the Almighty has brought misfortune upon me." (Ruth 1:20-21)

The name Naomi meant "lovely." There was nothing lovely about Naomi's life. No, her life had become "bitter," the very meaning of the name Mara. Anyone who has experienced a similar return home can relate to Naomi's feelings. You set out on a new phase of life with a heart full of dreams, only to return home with them shattered. It is easy to believe that God has forsaken you—that His hand is against you.

As Ruth stood next to Naomi, I wonder if Naomi's words hurt Ruth's heart. Naomi looked at the women of Bethlehem and plainly stated, "My life is empty." Think about how this must have felt to Ruth. Ruth had given up everything. She had given up her home, her family, and her gods. In response to Ruth's sacrificial love, Naomi made her feelings very clear: "I went away full, but the Lord has brought me back empty." (Ruth 1:21)

Determination in the face of despair

Determination—simply reading the word can fortify our faith. However, there is a difference between reading the word and exhibiting it in our daily walk with God. Godly determination requires strength that comes from the Lord. *Determination* is a firm or fixed intention to achieve a desired end.[ii] Determination is not an emotional whim that comes during the good times and exits during the hard times. Rather, determination is a resolve in our hearts and minds to live a certain way or to do a certain thing, no matter what. Determination requires persistence, self-discipline, and reliance on the Spirit of God for strength.

To me, one of the hardest times to display determination is when the people around me are negative. Maybe you know what it is like to have a family member or a close friend who serves up a constant dose of "hard reality." Based on the context of chapter one in the book of Ruth, we can conclude that Naomi was that type of person. Naomi told it like she saw it. The problem was that Naomi was in a bad place spiritually, which led her to see her circumstances from a negative point of view. This point of view affected her judgement, her outlook on life, and her view of God. As a result, Naomi discouraged Ruth from doing the very thing God called her to do.

Certainly, it would have been easy for Naomi to justify her negative feelings. She had been through famine, the death of her husband, the absence of grandchildren, and the death of her sons. We do not want to underestimate or fail to recognize the pain that was in Naomi's life. Anyone who has lost a loved one or gone through a long season of difficulty knows what it is like to simply try to make it through the day. They know what it is like to wonder if God has abandoned them.

I wonder if Naomi thought that she was doing Ruth a favor when she encouraged her to return to Moab? My instinct says that she did. Here is the important point. What Naomi thought was right turned out to be wrong. *In the midst of her pain, she lost sight of the greatness and goodness of God.*

When we lose sight of God's greatness and His goodness, we too find ourselves in a bad place spiritually. Our primary focus becomes the pain or challenge that is right in front of us. Temporary things like health, money, relationships, and careers become the basis by which we view God's character and ability. *This subtle switch happens when we allow our circumstances to determine how we view God's willingness and ability to work through us.*

In contrast, our view of God should be based on His character and His ability as taught in the Bible. We should always remember that God is the ultimate authority over our lives, directing the events of our lives, and fulfilling a plan through our lives. When these beliefs are firm in our hearts and minds, we are protected from ever-changing emotions based on the circumstances of life. The bottom line is this: When we embrace a view of God that is based on the Bible, we position ourselves to filter the circumstances of life in a productive way. *Instead of allowing our circumstances to determine the character of God, we allow the character of God to determine how we view our circumstances.* Naturally, this type of living requires determination.

Thankfully, Ruth chose to follow the road God had for her. She displayed determination even in the midst of a highly emotional situation that was born out of intense pain, hardship, and loss. Ruth's determination allowed her to make spiritual progress in her walk with God. Through all this she embraced:

- Hope instead of despair.
- Peace instead of strife.
- Power instead of weakness.

Romans 15:13 speaks about the reality of God's work in a believer's faith journey. This verse says, "**May the God of hope fill you with all joy and peace as you trust in him so that you may overflow with hope by the power of the Holy Spirit**." God's hope, peace, and power are not reserved for times when life is good or the circumstances of life are in our favor. Instead, they are available to us during every season of life, even the difficult ones. Let's examine Romans 15:13 and see how we can live a determined life in Christ.

Hope instead of despair

Hope. Believers in Jesus Christ always have a reason to hope. The very fact that God allows us to walk on His earth and breathe His air points us to a place of hope. Hope changes everything because it positions us to see all the ways that God is at work in our lives even during the difficult seasons.

This world is full of pain and loss. No one is immune. We all face situations that leave us asking, "Why, Lord?" A big-picture perspective develops when we embrace the fact that there is more going on in us and around us than what we can see. Big-picture living produces hope because at the core is the belief that this world is not our home—it never has been and it never will be.

In Romans 15:13 we learn about hope. It says, "**May the God of hope…**" Let's stop right there and consider this. We serve the God of hope. No other god offers life-changing or life-sustaining hope. There is only one God that produces hope. He is the living God who spoke all things into existence. He is the God of Abraham, Isaac, Jacob, Naomi, Ruth, and the God of you and me.

Biblical hope is more than a feeling. It is more than a desire for life to turn out the way we planned. Biblical hope is trustful expectation, particularly with reference to the fulfillment of God's promises.[iii] Hope is at the core of the Christian faith. Knowing that God has a plan and that He is always fulfilling His plan provides hope.

Believers in Jesus Christ have hope because of three important events.

First, there is Jesus' resurrection from the grave. Jesus died the death that we deserve. The moment that Jesus rose from the grave, sin and death were defeated. Because this world is plagued by sin, things like death, disease, and dismay continue to exist. However, Jesus accomplished the ultimate victory over all evil on the cross. Jesus' life, death, and victory over the grave paved the way for you and me to have a personal relationship with God that is based on eternity and not on the temporary things of this world.

Second, there is the indwelling of the Holy Spirit. The very presence of God lives inside of us. God's Spirit reminds us that we are His children and that we do not face any situation in life, whether hard or easy, on our own.

Third, there is God's gift to us of the Bible, which is full of His instructions as well as promises that we can claim. These promises are real and applicable to our daily walk with God. When we do not know what to do, God's Word provides direction. As we claim the promises that are in God's Word, hope flows into us.

The best way to nurture a sense of hope is to understand the greatness and goodness of God. The greatness of God is seen in God's mighty works throughout history. As we think about God's story we see how every prophecy in the Old Testament was fulfilled, how every important event in the New Testament was accomplished, and how every aspect of our lives fits into a bigger picture. The goodness of God is seen in God's loving attention to the details of life. Even though bad things happen, we serve a good God who is willing and able to bring beauty out of the ashes. Whether it is a marriage that is falling apart, a wayward child who is far from home, a friendship that is broken, a financial problem that has no solution, a diagnosis that is hopeless, a dream that is shattered, or a death that came too soon, God is good, and He is able to lovingly put our lives back together again.

How can God be great and good in the middle of trials and heartbreak? There is only one way. *God is a restoring God.* He brings purpose to our pain and meaning out of our mess. When faced with a difficult circumstance or a heartbreaking loss, we have a choice to make. Will we embrace the greatness and goodness of God by allowing Him to restore our lives, or will we embrace despair by allowing our circumstances to destroy us? I find it interesting that the definition for *despair* is to no longer have any hope or belief that a situation will improve or change.[iv] Despair wreaks havoc in a believer's life because it leaves no room for God and His restoring work. Naomi could have easily fallen into despair because she believed there was no hope for her. (Ruth 1:12-13, 20-21)

Embracing God means embracing hope. Hope reminds us that God is great and that He is good. Hope also reminds us that this world is not our home, and that restoration and healing are possible in Jesus' name. Unfortunately, these Biblical truths do not take away the sting of death, the pain of a shattered dream, or the heaviness of a difficult circumstance. Certainly, we still have to deal with real emotions as we walk the long road to our eternal home. However, truth, as recorded in the Bible, produces hope. Hope gives us a reason to be determined in our walk with God; we serve the God of hope!

Peace instead of strife

Peace. Believers in Jesus Christ have the opportunity to experience peace, even during overwhelming circumstances. Peace is a powerful reality in a believer's life, even during the darkest days. Peace comes when we choose to believe that God is with us even when life is against us. The good news about peace is this: Biblical peace is not dependent on a checklist of positive circumstances like a full bank account, a clean bill of health, a mended relationship, or a perfect record. No. Biblical peace comes from God and is dependent upon God.

Romans 15:13 provides important insight into godly peace. "May the God of hope **fill you with all joy and peace...**" *Real joy and peace originate with the God of hope*. When we understand that God is the source of hope, we are positioned to experience His joy and peace.

In this verse, the words *fill* and *with* come from one Greek word that means "to fill up."[v] This conveys the idea of a house being saturated with an aroma to the point where no space or area is untouched. It is reassuring to know that we have the opportunity to be filled up with God's joy and peace to the point where every single area of our lives is impacted and changed.

Knowing the Biblical definitions for joy and peace help us to base our lives on truth. This lets us make wise choices when our human emotions tempt us to veer off course.

Biblical *joy* is "the happy state that results from knowing and serving God. Joy is the fruit of a right relationship with God. Joy is not something people create by their own efforts."[vi] To experience godly joy, we must focus on Jesus. There must be a day-in-and-day-out walk with the Lord that is based on knowing, loving, and serving Him. This type of focus brings a sense of joy that is directly proportional to our focus on Jesus. The bottom line is this: the more we focus on Jesus, the more joy we will experience in our daily walk with Him. (Philippians

4:4, Galatians 5:22)

Biblical *peace* is "a sense of well-being and fulfillment that comes from God and is dependent on His presence."[vii] Peace is not the absence of problems but rather an assurance that God is with us. He is willing and able to meet our needs. He is willing and able to take care of our hearts. He is willing and able to use our challenging circumstances for our good. When we know that God is willing and able to work in our lives, we experience a sense of peace that cannot be explained.

As we trust in Him, we are filled with God's joy and peace. Romans 15:13 shows the connection between joy, peace, and trust. It states, "May the God of hope fill you with all joy and peace **as you trust in him**..."

Simply put, as we trust in God, we place our confidence in God and His ability to lead us. I will be honest—complete trust in God is hard for me. Everything inside of me longs to be in control. I especially want to be in control of the areas of life that matter the most to me. Trust, in the truest sense of the word, is when we surrender control of the areas that matter the most to us by saying, "Lord, not my will be done, but Your will be done." When we surrender at this level, we trust deeply by expressing our confidence in God and His willingness to lead us.

Trusting God during times of hardship can be a daunting task. When we try to express trust with our mouths, our hearts may be screaming, "Why, Lord?" "What is going to happen?" "How can I ever trust you again?" I believe that God is patient with us during these moments. He sees our need. He knows our pain. He understands our hardship. And He offers His unfailing love through it all. Trust is hard even on a good day. However, Scripture is clear. We are to trust God no matter what.

When we fail to trust God with the details of life, including the difficult ones, we often experience strife in our hearts and homes. *Strife* is a "very angry or violent disagreement between two or more people."[viii] Strife can make its way into our relationship with God. We may question God until our hearts become cold to Him. We simply do not care about God or the way He longs to work in our lives. Strife with God always leads to bitterness with others. We may grow bitter because the people around us are not meeting our needs in the way that we want them to be met. Or, we may grow bitter because the people around us are living the lives that we long to live.

In order to deal with strife that leads to bitterness, we need to focus on trusting God. One way to produce trust in our walk with God is to purposefully recognize all the ways that God is at work in our lives. Certainly trusting God requires determination. We have to actively engage in the trusting process. We have to make the choice to turn our cries of "Why, Lord?" into pleas of "Help me!" This determination to cling to God brings joy and peace, even when our circumstances don't seem to improve. Naomi's life provides a perfect example for us. God worked in, around, and through Naomi. As a result, we will see a vast change in her outlook on life. You will want to keep your eye on this part of the story line....

Power instead of weakness

Power. Believers in Jesus Christ have the opportunity to experience life-changing power. Life-changing power is a unique type of power that comes from the indwelling of the Spirit of God. There is not a single believer who is excluded from experiencing God's life-changing power. In fact, every believer in Jesus Christ has an infinite power supply housed inside of them. We know this because the same power that brought Jesus out of the grave resides in the heart and life of everyone who believes. (Ephesians 1:19)

Romans 15:13 talks about God's life-changing power. "May the God of hope fill you with all joy and peace as you trust in him, **so that you may overflow with hope by the power of the Holy Spirit**." The word *power* that is used here means, "to be able."[ix] For just a moment, allow this definition to sink in. In the face of overwhelming situations that leave you asking, "How can I move forward in my walk with God?" God has placed power in your life that answers simply, "You are able!" This God-given power reaches to the deepest places in our hearts and addresses the questions in our minds.

Questions like:
  "How can I trust again?"
    God says, "You are able!"
  "How can I recover from this event?"
    God proclaims, "You are able!"
  "How can I move on?"
    God states, "You are able!"

"How can I have hope for the future?"
God promises, "You are able!"

According to the Bible, our ability to move forward in life has nothing to do with self-will, the power of positive thinking, or pretending that the past never happened. Rather, this ability comes through embracing the power of the Holy Spirit. Besides empowering us, the role of the Holy Spirit is to lead, guide, protect, teach, and remind us.

An important step in accessing the power of God's Spirit is to recognize that we do not have the necessary strength to accomplish God-size tasks. Our sinful condition, along with our circumstances, renders us powerless. In and of ourselves, we are weak. *Weakness* is the "quality or feature that prevents someone or something from being effective or useful."[x] While weakness is a reality that we often face, we do not have to stay in a place of weakness. Our weakness can actually become our greatest strength.

Jesus said, "My grace is sufficient for you, for my power is made perfect in weakness." (2 Corinthians 12:9) In response Paul proclaimed, "Therefore I will boast all the more gladly about my weaknesses, so that Christ's power may rest on me. That is why, for Christ's sake, I delight in weaknesses, in insults, in hardships, in persecutions, in difficulties. For when I am weak, then I am strong." (2 Corinthians 12:10-11)

Each day we have a choice to make. Will we remain in our weakness and be made useless, or will we embrace God's life-changing power and be made able? Accessing God's life-changing power is not an easy task. Often it requires us to accept difficult realities. Maybe it is a death of a loved one, a financial circumstance that is hard to face, or a character issue that we need to address.

When we get real with God and with ourselves, this positions us to access God's life-changing power. *In order to make spiritual progress, we have to accept the truth.* Truth allows us to recognize our weakness and address the areas of life that are broken. It is from the place of truth that we hear the gentle voice of God saying, "My child, with My power, you are able."

Praise God that we do not have to face life on our own! God's Spirit goes before us, comes behind us, and gives us the strength that we need to move on in Jesus' name. As we move on, we demonstrate

God's life-changing power, which is more than able to meet our needs and move us forward in our walk with God. Naomi had to make the choice. Would she remain in her weakness or would she embrace God's life-changing power in her life?

Our Journey

If you have heard the statement, "Hindsight is 20/20," it certainly applies to the story of Naomi and Ruth. Sitting in our comfortable chairs with our Bibles open and our fancy coffees in hand, it is easy to assess who was right and who was wrong. It would be easy for us to say, "I am going to live like Ruth." However, the applications of the teachings found in Naomi and Ruth's story are much more challenging. The truth of the matter is this—we can relate to both Naomi and Ruth. There are times when we walk in hope, peace, and power. There are also times when we walk in despair, strife, and weakness.

With this in mind, I want to ask you a personal question. It is a question that is between you and the Lord. Does your life tend to follow the pattern of Naomi or the pattern of Ruth? If Naomi, then you tend to feel hopeless about the condition of your life. You may even want to give up. Peace is missing from your walk with God, so you run from God instead of to God. This running causes strife in your relationship with God, who longs to be your safe place. This strife affects your relationship with others until you experience bitterness when others succeed or have an experience that you want to have. You feel tired and weak. You have no idea how to move forward. The idea of giving up or giving in seems like the only option. However, if you are following the pattern of Ruth, you know that the only way you will make it through your time on this earth is by believing that God is at work even when you do not know His plan.

No matter where you are in life, hang on! It is still possible for you to experience hope, peace, and power, but it will take determination. Let's apply the teaching found in Romans 15:13 to our walk with God.

Embracing hope instead of despair

Ruth had hope that the God of Israel was the One True God. Through Ruth's actions we see her life proclaim that God is great and that He is good. Ruth placed herself in a position where God could do a restoring work in her life. Ruth said to Naomi, "Don't urge me to leave you or to turn back from you. Where you go I will go, and where you stay I will stay." (Ruth 1:16) Whether Ruth was aware of it or not, she lived her life with a big picture perspective. Certainly there was more going on in Ruth's life than what she could see. As we sit here today, we have the benefit of knowing Ruth's entire story. Ruth placed herself in a position to be restored. As she did, hope came into her life. God had a plan for Ruth's life. This plan was not only to restore Ruth, but it was also to restore others.

- What situation(s) are you facing in life that seems hopeless?
- How would your view of this situation change if you embraced a big picture perspective to life? What would happen if you chose to believe there was more going on around you than what you could see?
- Do you believe that God can restore your life again?
- What tends to be a trigger for you in regards to despair? When you are in a place of despair, what are you believing about God?

Experiencing peace instead of strife

Naomi was essentially predicting a future of emptiness for Ruth – no relationships, no faith, no home. Ruth spoke truth into Naomi's life, "Your people will be my people and your God will be my God." (Ruth 1:16) Even if Ruth did not know how God would fill her life, I think she sensed that it would happen. My guess is that Ruth did not fully experience God's peace until later in her story. But the first sign of peace came on the road to Bethlehem and right in the middle of one of the most difficult seasons of her life.

- Do you believe it is possible to experience peace during difficult seasons?
- How would it change your life if you were filled with joy and peace?
- How does strife show up in your life? Are you at odds with God? With others?
- Are you jealous of other people and their lives? How does this affect your own joy and peace?

Demonstrating power instead of weakness

At her crossroads, Ruth faced the possibility of poverty and a future of being different from everyone around her. However, Ruth chose to push through any fear (as well as the urging of Naomi) as she made the decision to leave Moab and embrace Bethlehem. The power to make this decision did not come from Ruth alone– *God made her able*. Ruth said to Naomi, "May the Lord deal with me, be it ever so severely, if anything but death separates me from you." (Ruth 1:17) To me, this is a sign that Ruth recognized the power of God and walked in it.

- What is God calling you to do that you are unable to do in your own power?
- How can getting real with God and yourself help you to embrace God's life-changing power?
- Do you believe that God's power can make you able?

Conclusion

Dear friend, no matter how bleak your situation looks, God is willing and able to meet you at your greatest point of need. Ask God to show you the next step He wants you to take. Then, take it in Jesus' name and in Jesus' power! As you do, hope, peace, and power will make their way into your daily walk with God. No matter how overwhelming your situation appears to be, your life can proclaim, "My God is able!"

Right now, invite God's Word to speak truth into your life. One way that you can claim the truth found in the Bible is by praying God's Word back to Him. You can do this by putting a verse of Scripture in your own words or by inserting your name or circumstance into a verse. This exercise will help you to internalize God's Word at a deep level. Take a moment and claim Romans 15:13.

You can pray, "*God, You are my hope. You fill my life with joy and peace. I will trust in You. I know that my life can overflow with Your hope. This hope has nothing to do with my power or ability. Rather, this hope has everything to do with the power of your Spirit who make me able.*" (Paraphrased)

Chapter 3
Engaging in Life

Her Journey

The barley harvest took place during the spring, marking a time of renewal. It is not a coincidence that Naomi and Ruth returned to Bethlehem at the beginning of the harvest. Even though Naomi and Ruth were at a low point in life, God was at work. He was positioning them for healing and restoration. Life-changing hope was never out of reach.

Remember how the nation of Israel fell into a cycle of sin, consequences, and restoration? As Naomi and Ruth returned to Bethlehem, we do not know where the nation was in its cycle with God. It is hard to know the spiritual condition of the people at this point in the story. *However, no matter what was going on in the hearts and lives of the people, God was present, and He was providing.* The people of Bethlehem must have been excited about the approaching harvest. The famine, only a few years before, was probably fresh in their memories. If you have been through a "famine," you know how grateful you are when God provides a "feast"!

As Naomi and Ruth returned to Bethlehem, they returned to a place that was full of life and activity. Harvest time was a busy time. Everyone in the community took part in the process. Gathering, threshing, winnowing, and storing the barley were familiar activities for the people of Bethlehem.

Large machinery and refined harvesting processes were not available in Naomi and Ruth's day. Gathering was exhausting work. Men and women walked through the fields and hand-picked the stalks of barley. Once picked, the barley was taken to the threshing floor where the stalks were removed. An animal pulled a threshing sled over the barley, or workers used sticks to beat the stalks. Winnowing was next. In the winnowing process, the dry outer casing of the barley called the chaff was removed. Large wooden forks were used to toss the barley in the air during the winnowing process. The dry outer casing blew away, and only the seed remained. Once the chaff was removed, the edible portion of the barley was stored in jars, cellars, small grain pits, larger silos, or stone houses until it was needed.[xi]

Barley was an important product in Ruth's day. It was a staple food for humans and animals. "Barley could be processed into a variety of products, including flour, flakes similar to oatmeal, and grits."[xii]

As the barley harvest began, Naomi and Ruth settled into life in Bethlehem. Scripture is quiet about the details; we are not told where they lived or how the people treated them once the shock of their return faded. What we do know is that the barley harvest provided a chance for them to collect grain, whether to store up for later or to meet their current needs. Maybe both! According to the Jewish laws found in Leviticus 19 and Deuteronomy 24, widows, foreigners, and the poor were entitled to collect whatever was left over after the bulk of the harvesting had been done. (In fact, landowners were instructed to not gather the gleanings but to leave them for others). These laws provided a glimpse into God's heart for the unlikely. They were never forgotten by their Heavenly Father.

At some point Ruth assessed the situation and began to make a plan. Ruth said to Naomi, "Let me go to the fields and pick up the leftover grain behind anyone in whose eyes I find favor." (Ruth 2:2) Naomi replied, "Go ahead, my daughter." (Ruth 2:2) Because of the Jewish laws, Ruth had every right to go to the field and ask to glean. Ruth left the place where she and Naomi lived. She came to a field and once again asked permission to pick up the leftover grain, and the foreman agreed.

Scripture notes an important detail here. "*As it turned out*, she was working in a field belonging to Boaz." (Ruth 2:3, italics added) The fact that Ruth found herself in Boaz's field was not an accident. In fact, prior to Ruth asking permission to glean, the author introduces us to Boaz. "Now Naomi had a relative on her husband's side, a man of standing from the clan of Elimelek, whose name was Boaz." (Ruth 2:1) With great literary style, the author set the stage for something extraordinary to take place.

Boaz arrived from Bethlehem and greeted his harvesters. Boaz said, "The Lord be with you!' 'The Lord bless you!' they answered." (Ruth 2:4) As the story unfolds, we will discover that Boaz is a key player, both in Ruth's journey and in God's plan of redemption.

Boaz looked around and, seeing Ruth, asked, "Who does that young woman belong to?" (Ruth 2:5) The person in charge replied, "She is the Moabite who came back from Moab with Naomi. She said, 'Please let me glean and gather among the sheaves behind the harvesters.' She came into the field and has remained here from morning till now, except for a short rest in the shelter." (Ruth 2:6-7)

It fascinates me that Boaz noticed Ruth. It could have been for several reasons. For example, she could have been noticeably different from everyone around her; maybe she did not look like the other women. Or it could also have been that he knew his workers and other people at the field, and Ruth was a stranger to him. No matter the reason, Ruth stood out to Boaz.

Imagine yourself in an unknown land and surrounded by unknown people. I wonder if Ruth thought, "Will I ever find a place to belong?" "What is going to happen to me?" No matter what questions filled Ruth's mind, she did not allow them to stop her from engaging in life. In the middle of an uncomfortable situation, Ruth displayed initiative. Ruth recognized the authority of others. And Ruth worked diligently until she completed her task.

Initiative, Authority, and Diligence

The life of Ruth demonstrates how initiative, authority, and diligence can work together. There will be times when we only need one or two of these qualities. Then there will be times when we need all three. *Ruth needed all three character qualities to move forward in her journey.* Let's take a closer look at the beautiful way that initiative, authority, and diligence can work together.

Initiative. Ruth displayed initiative when she identified the opportunity to glean. She knew that the barley harvest was taking place and that leftover grain would be available in the field. Ruth knew that she had the ability to pick up the grain and thresh it in order to provide food for herself and Naomi. Ruth did not wait for someone else to collect the grain. Ruth did not hide behind the excuse that, as a Moabite woman, she had no opportunity in Bethlehem. Instead, Ruth engaged in life.

Initiative involves recognizing a need (or opportunity) and formulating a plan in order to act on it. We display initiative in different ways and for different reasons. Let's discuss two types of initiative: godly initiative and selfish initiative.

Godly initiative results from a thought-out plan that is directed by the Holy Spirit. This type of initiative is displayed in a person who faithfully walks with God. Basic needs as well as complex needs are met through godly initiative. When we are cold, we seek shelter. When we are hungry, we find food. When we are lonely, we seek relationships.

If we want our daily walk to demonstrate godly initiative, the Bible will be our "go to" book for instruction. The Bible records God's story of love. We should never forget or take for granted that God lovingly preserved the Bible so that we can know how to live.

Psalm 119 is a unique chapter in the Bible. This psalm is made up of 176 verses. Each verse highlights an important aspect of following the instructions found in the Bible. For example, "I gain understanding from your precepts; therefore I hate every wrong path. Your Word is a lamp for my feet, a light on my path." (Psalm 119:104-5). To hate every wrong path is a lofty goal. Think about it. There are many paths that turn out to be wrong, but initially show up as right. How do we discover the discernment we need? The answer has at least two parts.

First, we need to trust God to reveal His plan to us. The Holy Spirit, our guide, lives inside of us. We never face a need, decision, or opportunity on our own. God faithfully shows us the actions that we need to take to fulfill His plan.

Second, we need to know that God has given us clear teachings in the Bible. *The Bible is vital because it gives us instructions for navigating through this dark world.* God's Word is the primary way that God speaks to His people, and it is a source of light directing us in the way we should live. God will never call us to do something that goes against the Bible. Therefore, spending time daily in God's Word prepares us to step out and display godly initiative.

Selfish initiative comes from selfish motives that are directed by our flesh, the part of us that is sinful and wants immediate satisfaction. This type of initiative is dangerous to our walks with God because we attempt to *satisfy a legitimate need in the wrong way.* Real needs can include comfort, purpose, direction, and love. If you have stepped outside of God's plan for your life by seeking to meet those needs in the wrong place or in the wrong way, you know what I am talking about. Here is one example: You are having a rough week and need reassurance. Certainly there is nothing wrong with this need. It is totally normal to want others to love and accept you. However, you might become driven to get reassurance from people rather than from God. You might try to earn a friend's affection by doing them a favor or to get praise from your boss by working extra hard. This can lead to a lot of initiative and activity in your life. *However, the initiative and activity are misguided and can actually hurt your walk with God.*

The reality of the matter is this: If we do not focus on the Lord by spending time with Him each day and filling our lives with God-given truth, we will easily fall into the trap of displaying selfish initiative instead of godly initiative.

"You were running a good race. Who cut in on you and kept you from obeying the truth?" (Galatians 5:7) In this verse the Apostle Paul spoke to the believers in Galatia who had turned from biblical truth and embraced a lie. These believers had gone from basing their salvation on Jesus' death, burial, and resurrection to adding the act of circumcision as a requirement for salvation. Their legitimate need for a relationship with God was tainted by their wrong beliefs about God and the way He worked in their lives. These wrong beliefs led to wrong actions and a compromised walk with God.

If you are wondering what type of initiative you display in your daily walk with God, take this easy test. Look at your actions and trace them back to your belief system. Ask yourself the question, "Why am I doing this?" Your answer should always match up with the teachings found in the Bible. If it does not, then stop what you are doing and ask God to redirect your steps.

Authority. Without a close look at Scripture, it would be easy to miss the important connection between godly initiative and authority. This connection is exciting, and I do not want you to miss it! The word *authority* refers to the power to give orders, make decisions, or direct someone or something.[xiii] We cannot exhibit godly initiative without understanding and accepting the role of authority in our lives. Godly initiative that is based on the guidance of the Holy Spirit and the Bible respects authority.

Once Ruth had a plan, she included Naomi – her authority figure– in the process. Stop and visualize the moment. Ruth went to Naomi before she left her house to glean. "Let me go to the fields and pick up the leftover grain behind anyone in whose eyes I find favor." (Ruth 2:2) For many of us the idea of asking permission is difficult to accept or is simply a step that is easily forgotten. We enjoy our independence, and our culture encourages us to do whatever we think is right. This independence becomes a problem when we step outside of God's line of authority. We do this by ignoring Him or the people that He has placed in positions of authority over us.

Our line of authority always begins with God. He created us, and we are His. God gives us purpose, direction, and meaning. Anyone who has placed their faith in Jesus for the forgiveness of their sins has proclaimed God's authority over his or her life.

Many benefits come from recognizing God's authority as well as the authority of others. We will discuss those benefits later in this chapter. First, let's look at two passages of scripture that show God's authority in action.

Prior to Jesus' death, He prayed for His disciples, "Holy Father, *protect* them by the *power of your name*, the name you gave me, so that they may be one as we are one." (John 17:11, emphasis added) When Jesus prayed, He asked that His followers be protected by the Name of God. In this request, Jesus connected the Name of God with the power of God.

Why would Jesus make this connection? The answer is tucked away in the Old Testament. Remember how God instructed Moses to return to Egypt in order to lead the Israelites out of captivity and into the promised land? In that conversation, God made it clear that His name carried great power. " Moses said to God, 'Suppose I go to the Israelites and say to them, "The God of your fathers has sent me to you," and they ask me, "What is his name?" Then what shall I tell them?' God said to Moses, '*I AM who I AM*. This is what you are to say to the Israelites: "*I AM* has sent me to you."'" (Exodus 3:13-14, emphasis added)

As the story unfolded, God demonstrated the power that was in His Name. What could the great I AM do? He could send plagues. He could part the Red Sea. He could provide water, quail, and manna. He could lead by a cloud during the day and a pillar of fire during the night. All of these actions displayed amazing power, the power that was (and is) housed in the very Name of God. "I AM who I AM!"

Let's put these truths together. God's name has always been associated with power. With power comes authority. There has never been a ruler who had great authority but no power. Conversely, there has never been a ruler who had great power but no authority. Why? Because power and authority always go together.

When Jesus prayed, "Holy Father, *protect* them by the *power of your name...*" Jesus was asking the Father to provide the type of protection that can only come from the all-knowing and all-seeing Creator of the universe. *It is important for us to understand and accept the truth that submitting to God's authority brings protection to our journey.* This protection comes from God calling us to take steps that are in line with His plan. (If you are wondering if you can trust God and His plan, Romans 12:2 defines God's plan as good, pleasing, and perfect. I can't think of a better reason to ask Him to direct our steps. He has a plan, and it is a great plan!)

In addition to God, other people in our lives represent lines of authority. Depending on our situation, our line of authority might involve a husband, a parent, a boss, or a ministry leader. While we do not treat these individuals like we treat God, we do respect them and the role God designed for them to play. (Of course, a few of these people we love with all of our hearts!)

When we treat the individuals who are in positions of authority over us with respect, we pave the way to experience the same type of unity that Jesus shared with His Father. Remember how John 17:11 says, "...so that they may be one as we are one." God longs for His children to be in unity with one another. This type of unity was demonstrated in the lives of Naomi and Ruth. Ruth included Naomi in her decision to glean. This action communicated respect for Naomi and the role she played in Ruth's life. Naomi and Ruth's journeys were deeply connected. Without Naomi, Ruth had no standing in Bethlehem. Without Ruth, Naomi had no hope of preserving her family lineage. The fact that Ruth involved Naomi in the decision to glean further unified these two women.

When Ruth went to Naomi and asked permission to glean, another benefit occurred. *Ruth set the stage for additional protection to come into her life.* Later in the story, we will see how Naomi was able to help Ruth stay safe in the fields. This protection could have been missing if Ruth had tried to go around Naomi's wishes or leave Naomi out of her decision. What can we learn from this? Before we set out on a new direction in life, we need to stop and talk to the individuals who are in authority over us. This action communicates respect to them and brings additional protection into our lives.

What are the benefits of accepting God's authority?

- When we embrace God's authority, we experience His protection.
- When we embrace God's authority, we experience His power.
- When we embrace God's authority, we experience His peace through unity with others.

Diligence. After we have stepped out in godly initiative and recognized the role of authority in the process, we are ready to work hard at the task God calls us to complete. Think back to Ruth. Once she was in the field, she worked steadily. Ruth's work ethic caught the attention of the field manager, who commented (maybe even bragged?) to Boaz about her. "She came into the field and has remained here from morning till now, except for a short rest in the shelter." (Ruth 2:7) Think of what might have happened to her reputation (and Naomi's) if the overseer had noticed her napping, flirting with the harvesters, or whining about the hard work!

Diligence is when we make a commitment not only to the task but also to the details required to complete the task. This means that we are willing to do the fun work as well as the not-so-fun work. *We need to avoid making an emotional commitment, such as giving a quick agreement to a task and then letting our enthusiasm dwindle over time.* For some of us, making an emotional commitment and then not following through is a constant temptation. To counter this tendency, it is important to remember that the way we work either honors the Lord or it does not.

In the New Testament, we see that the Apostle Paul recognized the value of diligence. Paul often included personal greetings in his letters to the early churches, and time and time again he affirmed the people who demonstrated diligence. At the conclusion of the book of Romans, Paul pointed out four women who worked hard. This greeting blesses my heart because Paul can have a bad reputation when it comes to his view on women. I think verses like these help to set the record

45

straight. Paul valued anyone who worked diligently for God's Kingdom. Paul stated, "Greet Mary, who *worked very hard for you.*" (Romans 16:6, italics added) "Greet Tryphena and Tryphosa, those women who *work hard* in the Lord. Greet my dear friend Persis, another woman who has *worked very hard* in the Lord." (Romans 16:12, italics added) I do not know what these women did, but I do know that they honored Jesus with their efforts. As a result, their hard work made an impact on the people around them.

Throughout the Bible, individuals who worked hard at the task God placed in front of them were affirmed. Today, the same principle applies. As we work hard, with our eyes focused on Jesus, we prepare to complete the task no matter how long it takes or how difficult it is. We become a living picture of how initiative, authority, and diligence fit together to move us forward in our walk with God.

Our Journey

God put Ruth in the right place, at the right time, and for a definite purpose. When Ruth set out to glean in the field that morning, she had no idea what God was about to do. She was simply trying to meet the need in her life. Little did Ruth know that her actions were preparing her to take a giant step forward in her walk with God.

Maybe you are at a point in life where all you can see is your immediate need. If so, hang on to this truth: *God is at work in your life.* He has brought you to the right place, at the right time, for a definite purpose. What can you do in your current situation? You can display godly initiative, establish God's authority over your life, and work hard at completing your task.

Initiative. Each day we have the opportunity to engage in life and become a part of finding a solution to the problems that we face. It is vital to examine the type of initiative that we display. *Godly initiative* is directed by the Holy Spirit as well as by the instructions found in the Bible. In this initiative, we wake up each day and invite the Lord to direct our steps. We ask Him to show us where to go, what to do, and how to embrace His plan for our day. Along the way, our needs are met.

In *selfish initiative*, we wake up and attempt to meet our needs in the wrong way. Whether it is the need to be accepted, affirmed, or wanted, we try to meet it our own way and for our own good. Selfish initiative hurts our walk with God because it tempts us to go against God and His Word to get what we want. Everyone gives in to selfish motives occasionally because none of us is perfect. However, selfish initiative is a slippery slope that leads us further and further away from God and His plan. In a life of selfish initiative, we are never truly satisfied. We find temporary satisfaction in affirmation or an opportunity, but we are never really changed. This lack of satisfaction leads us to take another selfish step.

Thankfully we do not have to be stuck in a life of selfish initiative. We can return to God and His Word. We serve a loving Father who daily extends the opportunity for us to begin again. This is one of my favorite passages that describes God's love for us. "The Lord is compassionate and gracious, slow to anger, abounding in love. He will not always accuse, nor will he harbor his anger forever; he does not treat us as our sins deserve or repay us according to our iniquities. For as high as the heavens are above the earth, so great is his love for those who fear him; as far as the east is from the west, so far has he removed our transgressions from us." (Psalm 103:8-12)

- What type of initiative do you typically display, godly or selfish?
- Think about a specific example.
- How do the Holy Spirit and God's Word help you to display godly initiative?
- How much time do you spend each day in prayer and Bible study?
- Why is it important to spend time with God each day? How does your personal time with Jesus impact your ability to walk with Him?
- Think about a time when you displayed selfish initiative. How did this lead to additional selfish steps?

Authority. Two benefits of daily submitting to God's authority come in the form of His protection and unity with other people in your life. First, when we daily submit to the authority of God, we find ourselves nestled into the plan of God. If you remember, we read earlier, "As it turned out, she was working in a field belonging to Boaz." (Ruth 2:3) As we obey God, we will also have "as it turned out" moments that will not be coincidences. Just like Ruth, we will find ourselves in the right place, at the right time, and fulfilling a definite purpose. These "as it turned out" moments are lovingly planned in the heart of God. Second, when we submit to the additional lines of authority, we experience a unique type of unity that provides additional protection.

Think about the role of authority:

- Do you struggle with submitting to God or to the people God has placed in positions of authority in your life? If so, how does this affect your walk with God?
- How can respecting the authority of leaders in your life strengthen your relationship with God and with them?
- Have you ever experienced an "as it turned out" moment? If so, how did God orchestrate that event? How does respecting God's authority in your life lead to this type of moment?

Diligence. For just a moment, think about how someone would describe your work ethic. Are you a diligent worker? Once you start a task, do you complete it? Or do you emotionally commit to something, only to allow your commitment to fade over time?

It is easy to fall into the trap of making an emotional commitment to a task. We start out strong, with lots of ideas and momentum. The task brings a sense of purpose and excitement. However, somewhere along the way, the momentum drops. This is the point when we can assess our work ethic. If you consistently push projects to the side without completing them, you may need to address this problem. You may need to look at your work ethic and ask the question, "Am I a hard worker?" If the pattern of your life is different, meaning that you typically complete a task (especially when you have to rely on God's strength to do so), then you demonstrate diligence.

- Think about the work God has called you to perform, whether that is as a wife, a mom, a professional, a student, or a mixture of these. Would you describe yourself as a hard worker?
- How do you respond when the work is hard to complete? Are you able to dig deep, lean on Jesus, and complete a task? If so, give an example.
- Can you think of a time when you made an emotional commitment to a task but were unable to complete it? What

48

did you learn from the experience? How can you avoid repeating this in the future?

Conclusion

God was at work in Ruth's life every step of the way, and even through the decisions and discussions and gleaning, God was providing! Ruth chose to engage in life. She did not give up or decide that all hope was lost. Instead, she set out to make the best of her circumstances, and as she did, she discovered that God had orchestrated a beautiful solution. Think about this: *God's ability to provide always exceeds our level of need.* Always. If you are in a place where your need is great, hold on to this truth. No matter how overwhelming your circumstances are, praise God for His ability to work in and through you. Your Heavenly Father is calling you to walk in confidence with him. Along the way, God will help you to display godly initiative, establish authority over your life, and work hard to complete the task before you. It will take determination to do what this chapter encourages you to do. Do not give up! Do not fall short! Engage in life as you press on with all your God-given might!

Chapter 4
Finding a Safe Place

Her Journey

Ruth was gleaning in the field when a man walked up to her and began a conversation. "Boaz said to Ruth, 'My daughter, listen to me. Don't go and glean in another field and don't go away from here. Stay here with the women who work for me. Watch the field where the men are harvesting, and follow along after the women. I have told the men not to lay a hand on you. And whenever you are thirsty, go and get a drink from the water jars the men have filled.' " (Ruth 2:8-9)

Boaz showed concern for Ruth by giving instructions for her safety as well as protectively calling her his daughter. Ruth was at a place in her life where she had to listen to others and trust them. This put her in a vulnerable position. Like us, Ruth had the choice to believe that God had provided a safe place for her.

It makes me smile to think of what a "Pinch me, I'm dreaming!" moment this could have been for her. Ruth set out that morning not knowing where to go or what kind of response she would receive. Would she find a field? Would she be granted permission to glean? Would she be safe while out in the fields? God provided the answers. Not only did God guide her to this certain field, the owner himself chose to speak peace into her life.

"At this, she bowed down with her face to the ground. She asked him, "Why have I found such favor in your eyes that you notice me—a foreigner?" (Ruth 2:10) Ruth lived with the weight of being an outsider. She knew what it felt like to not belong. Ruth carried the stigma of being a Moabite. God's feelings about the Moabite people were summed up in Deuteronomy 23:3: "No Ammonite or Moabite or any of their descendants may enter the assembly of the Lord, not even in the tenth generation." There was a long, uncomfortable history between the nation of Israel and the nation of Moab. In Numbers 22 and 23 the King of Moab attempted to hire a pagan prophet to speak a curse over God's people, but the prophet ended up speaking a blessing instead.

It is impossible for us to know how Ruth was treated day-in-and-day-out in Bethlehem. In any case, she had attracted some notice. She stood out, and her story stood out. Boaz made it clear to Ruth that he knew about her and the sacrifice she had made for Naomi. "'I've been told all about what you have done for your mother-in-law since the death of your husband—how you left your father and mother and your homeland and came to live with a people you did not know before.'" (Ruth 2:11) Don't forget that earlier in the story Naomi proclaimed to the women of Bethlehem, "I went away full, but the Lord has brought me back empty." (Ruth 1:21) With that statement Naomi dismissed the sacrifice that Ruth made when she moved to Bethlehem. In contrast, God provided encouragement for Ruth through Boaz, whose words assured her, "I see you and I see what you have done!"

The outside is a hard and lonely place to live. It can leave you feeling like you have to do all the "right things" to earn acceptance. You feel like no one thinks you're worth including. You may bury yourself in busyness so you don't have to deal with the bigger issue of loneliness. If nothing changes, you end up stuck on the sidelines or tiptoeing through life, trying to go unnoticed.

Boaz not only noticed Ruth, he also blessed her. "'May the Lord repay you for what you have done. May you be richly rewarded by the Lord, the God of Israel, under whose wings you have come to take refuge.'" (Ruth 2:12) At some point in Ruth's life, she found her refuge in the God of Israel; a Moabite woman found her safe place in her relationship with the One True God. The word *refuge* that Boaz used in verse twelve to describe Ruth's relationship with God means to *trust in, confide in, and hope in someone.*[xiv] Ruth's actions showed Boaz and others the condition of her heart, both in her journey to Bethlehem and in the barley field.

When Boaz spoke to her, Ruth did not act like she did not need his help, and she did not try to repay him. Instead, Ruth answered, "'May I continue to find favor in your eyes, my lord.... You have put me at ease by speaking kindly to your servant—though I do not have the standing of one of your servants.'" (Ruth 2:13) Slowly, she was drawn in by Boaz and his grace. She got a taste of life on the inside. Perhaps Ruth began to hope there could be a future for her in Bethlehem.

Grace, Humility, and Refuge

Grace. Getting something we don't deserve... or not getting something we do deserve. Grace. In its simplest form, it's God's favor. Grace is a gift and is never based on what we do or try to do. Grace starts with God and is credited to our lives when we believe in Jesus.

Grace is at the heart of Ruth's story. Think back through the chapters. Ruth DID NOT deserve to be treated by Boaz as one of his servant girls, yet she was. Ruth DID deserve to be treated as an outsider, yet she was not.

Grace changes the direction of our lives. It moves us from the outside to the inside. Nothing brings more confidence into our daily walk with God than receiving the grace He extends to us. At the same time, receiving grace is not always easy.

If you are like me, you know what it is like to struggle in your relationships. Whether it is our relationship with God, with others, or both, it is tempting to try to go through life on our own. Sometimes lies work their way into our lives, and we find ourselves believing them. These lies make it hard for us to accept grace in our walk with Christ.

Have you ever believed the lie that you are a burden to the people around you? This lie whispers that every move that you make disappoints or bothers others. Instead of walking in the confidence of who God created you to be, you try to go unnoticed. You spend a lot of time and energy trying to avoid making mistakes. You try to make sure that you do everything "just right." In the end, you are paralyzed by fear, unsure of which move to make. A life of second-guessing your actions leaves you exhausted and always thinking that you have to do more in order to measure up.

Have you ever believed the lie that you have to pay people back for their kindness? This is a hard way to live because you spend a lot of time and energy trying to keep score. You spend your days thinking, "If they do this for me, then I have to do that for them." Before long, pulling away from people is easier than keeping score every day. You isolate yourself and do your best to meet your needs with your own resources.

Have you ever believed the lie that you are stuck on the outside? When you struggle with this lie, you believe you have nothing to offer, and others wouldn't miss you if you left. Consciously or unconsciously, you exclude yourself from groups. Often this is in subtle actions; perhaps you are inconsistent in making plans with others, or you send mixed messages. You may shut down emotionally, or shut others out because you expect every friendship to fail. You may get involved in so many different activities that you may appear to have no room in your life for others. Unfortunately, it is so normal (and acceptable) to have an overflowing schedules that we don't even realize it can be a spiritual issue.

In the middle of these lies, we have a choice to make. We can accept what these lies say about us, or we can believe the truth. If we think about Ruth's story, we can see where the same lies could have tempted her. Think how easy it would have been for Ruth to feel like a burden to the people around her. Ruth had no way to provide for herself. She was a Moabite woman living in the land of Israel. Ruth had no land and probably very little money once she left Moab. As a result, Ruth had to accept the kindness of others even though she could not pay them back. As for being an outsider, she was different from the other women in Bethlehem. Through marriage to an Israelite, her move to Israel, and her faith in the One True God, she became different from the Moabite women back home, too.

Despite these harsh realities, Ruth accepted grace. She showed humility by admitting that she needed help. Ruth then had to make sure that she received help from the right sources in her life.

We express humility each time we recognize that we need help. While it may be tempting to try, we cannot expect to live life on our own. Trying to solve all our problems alone has roots in pride. In contrast, challenges give us an opportunity to show a humility that honors the Lord. Letting ourselves be vulnerable with God and with others actually helps us grow in maturity. Expressing humility by looking for refuge in the right places is a crucial aspect of our daily walk with God.

Humility. *Humility* is when we show dependence on God and respect for others.[xv] When we demonstrate humility, we know that we are not better or worse than the people around us. Scripture makes this point clear. All humans are in the same boat: "All have sinned and fall

53

short of the glory of God." (Romans 3:23) Every person is affected by sin. Sin happens each time that we think, act, or react in a way that is offensive to God. Sin separates us from God, and there is no human remedy for the sin problem that plagues us. As a result, all of us know what it is like to be a burden, to be in need of help that we cannot repay, and to be stuck on the outside.

Refuge. The idea of refuge is best understood in the context of danger. We run to a refuge when we sense we cannot take care of ourselves. Every person longs for a refuge, a safe place where we are wanted, welcomed, and protected. Because of sin, we are in need of a spiritual safe place. According to Scripture, this is found in Jesus. "Therefore, since we have been justified through faith, we have peace with God through our Lord Jesus Christ, through whom we have gained access by faith into this grace in which we now stand." (Romans 5:1-2)

The safe place for you and me is the place of grace. It is the place where we are protected from the consequences of sin. Thankfully, getting to this safe place is not dependent on us. God works in our hearts and reveals to us that we need a Savior. We then have the opportunity to respond in faith. (John 6:37,44) Scripture explains clearly that we are made right with God through the process of faith. This faith means believing what God said is true. At the heart of the Christian message we find one resounding truth: God loves you and sent His Son to die for you!

When we trust God by placing our faith in Jesus' death on the cross, we enter our spiritual safe place. An important part of this process is understanding that we cannot earn our way or repay God for the grace that He extends. We simply have to humble ourselves and receive God's grace as a gift.

As Jesus hung on the cross, He bore the consequences of our sin. He paid the penalty for every wrong thought, action, and reaction that ever happened. The moment that Jesus rose from the grave, He proclaimed victory over our sin burden and everything that forces us to live on the outside. When we place our faith in Jesus and His work on the cross, we have peace with God. We are no longer on the outside, we are included in the family of God. This is a huge example of receiving something that we do not deserve! Through Jesus, we gain access into the place of grace—a place that provides hope, healing love, and peace.

When the burden of sin is removed, we find freedom. We are no longer limited to living in a place of shame and fear. We are no longer blind to the worth that God places on our lives. We can stop tiptoeing through life trying to go unnoticed. We can accept the truth that God is love and that He willingly gives grace to us.

The result? We begin to live—really live! This is thanks to the truth found in the next part of Romans 5. "You see, at just the right time, when we were still powerless, Christ died for the ungodly. Very rarely will anyone die for a righteous person, though for a good person someone might possibly dare to die. But God demonstrates his own love for us in this: While we were still sinners, Christ died for us." (Romans 5:6-8)

The journey from the outside to the inside is simple, yet profound. It is simple enough for the smallest child to understand yet profound enough to baffle the brightest scholar. God sent Jesus to die so that we can truly live. Jesus died so that we can have hope, peace, and power, right in the middle of our ordinary days. He allows us to live at peace with ourselves as well as others. Most importantly, Jesus' death, burial, and resurrection allow us to live at peace with God.

Our Journey

Here is an all-important question: Have you placed your faith in Jesus?

If so, thank Jesus for His life-changing work!

If not, this is a crucial application point. Recognize the fact that you have sin is in your life and that the consequence for sin is serious. Sin separates you from God, both on earth and for eternity.

If you are ready, you can ask Jesus to save you right now. You do not have to be in a church or even with another person. Thank Jesus for His death, burial, and resurrection, and believe the Bible when it says that Jesus' death was enough to pay your sin debt. Then place your faith in Jesus Christ as your Lord. Talk to God and discover how simple it is to move from the outside, which is separation from God, to the inside, which is a life-changing relationship with God! When Jesus comes into your life and saves you, you show humility by seeking proper refuge. You recognize your need for a Savior, and you surrender to that need. You place your trust, confidence, and hope in

Jesus. As you take this all-important step, you can be certain of this fact: God is at work in your life. You are turning to God and finding refuge in Him because He is faithfully calling you to Himself.

Once we establish Jesus as our spiritual safe place, we are ready to examine our willingness to show humility by finding refuge with the people God places in our lives. This, more than any other character quality in Ruth, makes an impact on me. Ruth needed the people God placed in her life. Because Ruth had a relationship with the One True God, she was able to be vulnerable with the people around her in a way that helped her on her faith journey.

Humility

As much as we may want to, we are not able to walk through life on our own. God places people in our lives at different times and for different reasons. Daily, God invites us to trust Him by going to a place of vulnerability with others.

When Ruth set out on that morning to find a field where she could glean, she was dependent on God to lead her steps. Ruth was also dependent on the help of people in Bethlehem. My question for you is this: do you daily recognize that you need help from the people God places in your life? Have you ever realized that we also need earthly relationships that provide a safe place?

Jesus provides the ultimate safe place. Like Ruth, we need to find our refuge in our relationship with the Lord. Then we will have a strong foundation to build our lives upon, and we can open up to others. Until our safe place with Jesus is established, every other safe place will fall short of meeting the ultimate need for relationship in our lives. Once we have the vertical relationship with God right, our horizontal relationships with others can meet the need they are designed to meet. Otherwise we will look to them for things we were never supposed to find there.

Because Ruth found safety in her relationship with God, she was able to go to a place of vulnerability and trust with Boaz. This is a crucial point for us to understand. When God is our ultimate safe place, we are able to trust others at a deeper level. Why? Because our confidence is NOT based on the actions or reactions of the people around us. It's based on our relationship with Jesus and His life-changing work.

Think about this: even though Ruth did not know Boaz, she

expressed a willingness to trust him. This willingness enabled Ruth to push past any lie that might have plagued her mind. Ruth resisted the urge to believe that she was a burden, that she had to repay a kindness, or that she was stuck on the outside.

God puts people in our lives at different times and for different reasons—people who willingly provide a safe place for us. These people love us, want God's best for us, encourage us in our walk, and want us to be an active part of their life, too. Sometimes it is hard to trust others. Often this struggle comes from rejection in the past, pain in our current situation, or fear of the future. If we do not recognize how our past rejection, present pain, or future fear affects us, it will be hard for us to trust the people God places in our lives. It's important for us to find refuge in the Lord and with others if we want to make spiritual progress.

Refuge

First, we can find refuge in the Lord. Through Bible study, prayer, worship, and accountability we can learn how to find refuge in the Lord. This is an important step because it protects us from trying to find our identity and meaning from the people or relationships in our lives. Learning to find refuge in the Lord is a long and sometimes slow spiritual journey. For a season of life, it may be necessary to really focus on the Lord by cultivating a strong relationship with Him. Limiting time with others and increasing time in the Bible can be helpful as we seek God's Word and clear direction.

As a note of caution, limiting contact with others to focus on God is different than limiting contact out of a fear of rejection. Think back to your school days. Most of us stood on the wall at one point or another waiting to be picked for a team. As we stood there, we thought, "Pick me, pick me, pick me!" This same longing shows up in our adult lives, just in more sophisticated ways. Whether it is a job promotion, a fun evening out with friends, or an invitation to be a part of something special, we yearn to be chosen. We can so easily run to relationships and experiences in order to feel wanted, welcomed, and protected. We may even manipulate situations to get what we want. Years or decades later, memories of times we were rejected, ignored, or forgotten still hurt.

Throughout the Bible, God repeats His answer to our search for refuge. *You are wanted, He says. You are welcomed. You are chosen.*

You do not have to manipulate any more. Your standing in Christ is secure. Your identity and purpose are based on your relationship with Me.

Second, we can find refuge with others. Do you remember the lies we discussed earlier in this chapter? Let's see if we can answer these lies with truths. If we believe that we are a burden to others, we will keep people at arm's length. *A life as a burden does not have to be our reality.* Instead of believing that lie, we can know that God created us to be a blessing. We can know that God loves us and has a plan for us. Also, God often puts people in our lives who want to help us when we have problems. Accepting this help does not make us weak or needy... it makes us real. Being real is refreshing. When we are real, we see that the relational walls in our lives can, by God's grace, slowly begin to fall.

If we believe that we have to repay a kindness with an equal or greater kindness, we will constantly be keeping score. *A life of keeping score does not have to be our reality.* Instead of believing that lie, we can simply receive the grace that God and others extend to us. We can say, "Thank you." No strings attached. This does not mean that we will not extend a kindness to others in their time of need. Of course we will! However, the motivation for kindness will be different. Instead of keeping score, we will start loving others and allowing them to love us.

If we believe that we will always be stuck on the outside, we shut ourselves away from others. *A life on the outside does not have to be our reality.* Instead of believing that lie, we can remind ourselves that we belong to the family of God. When invited to take part in a group, we can accept. When others offer to help when we have a need, we can let them help. We can choose to avoid the tendency to overthink invitations or second-guess motives. Instead, we can simply accept the opportunity to be included in the lives of others.

Remember, it is important for you to put yourself in the position to be a blessing, to share kindness, and to be included. Join a small group or Bible study at your church. Look for opportunities to take part in social or community organizations that are honoring to the Lord. Get involved in the lives of others, and invite others to get involved in your life, too. Stop hiding and stop running. You are not that person anymore. Instead, start living.

- Where do you look for refuge? Is it hard for you to place your trust in God? If so, how is this affecting you?

- Make a list of the people who are meaningfully involved in your life. I like to call this a "pour in" list. These are the people who consistently "pour into" your life. These are the people who love you, want God's best for you, encourage you in your walk, and want you to be an active part of their life, too. As you develop your list, write out the God-given role that each person plays. Thank God for the people on your list. Let them know—through a phone call, coffee date, or message—the important role that they play in your life as well as in your walk with God.
- Do you struggle with any of the relational lies described in this chapter? If so, how does this lie affect your relationship with God and others?
- If, after reading this chapter, you placed your faith in Jesus by asking Him to save you from your sins, tell a friend or ministry leader. Get involved at a church that teaches the Bible. Know that there is rejoicing in Heaven!

Conclusion

Why should we trust the Lord during difficult times? Because He has proven His love by sending His Son, Jesus. Through one act of love, God provided a spiritual safe place for us. *This safe place is so strong that no tragedy can take it, and no doubt should shake it.*

If you long to move from the outside to the inside, run to Jesus. You will find that His grace is already at work in you. This grace will change the direction of your life, you will know what it is like to be wanted, welcomed, and protected.

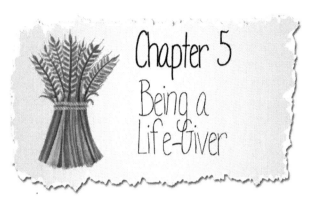

Chapter 5
Being a Life-Giver

Her Journey

Imagine Ruth's surprise when Boaz invited her to take a break from gleaning so that she could join him for a meal. Soon she found herself sitting with the harvesters and eating roasted grain in addition to bread that she dipped in wine vinegar. If you have ever been hungry due to a time of "famine" in your own life, and a meal is provided beyond what you expect, you can relate to Ruth's experience. Ruth ate until she was full and even had food to spare. It makes me smile to see the length and breadth of God's willingness to satisfy Ruth's needs!

Gleaning continued after the meal. Whether Ruth knew it or not, Boaz gave special instructions to his harvesters. "Let her gather among the sheaves and don't reprimand her. Even pull out some stalks for her from the bundles and leave them for her to pick up, and don't rebuke her." (Ruth 2:15-16) Do you remember the Hebrew word *hesed* from earlier in the book? *Hesed* meant mercy and faithfulness, especially to one less fortunate. It's a concept that is central to Ruth's story as well as to our own. The instructions that Boaz gave to the harvesters went above and beyond what the law required him to do. According to the Jewish law, landowners only had to leave the leftover grain for the less fortunate. Boaz did not want Ruth to just pick up whatever grain was left over; he wanted her to glean from an abundant supply! This was *hesed* in action.

Ruth gleaned and gleaned and gleaned. Once the gleaning was complete, Ruth threshed the barley. The threshing process involved removing the stalk from the barley and preparing it for further processing. Ruth had lots of barely to process. In modern measurements, she gleaned between thirty to fifty pounds of barley in one day.

Boaz had blessed Ruth through his act of *hesed*, and she did not miss the chance to pass on the blessing. Ruth returned home and presented the barley to Naomi, along with the food that was left over from her meal. Naomi's response? "Where did you glean today? Where did you work? Blessed be the man who took notice of you!" (Ruth 2:19) Naomi knew that something extraordinary must have taken place during Ruth's day. For the first time in Scripture we sense hope and excitement in Naomi's words.

I wish we could go back in time and hear the conversation that took place between Naomi and Ruth. Up to this point in the story, every recorded conversation (as well as every life event) had been hard. Finally, we see Naomi and Ruth basking in a happy moment. What a breath of fresh air this must have been for this duo!

As Ruth shared the details of her day with Naomi, the identity of the landowner was mentioned. As a newcomer to Bethlehem, Ruth might not have attached any significance to it, explaining, "The name of the man I worked with today is Boaz." (Ruth 2:19) Naomi was delighted to hear this news. She even proclaimed a blessing over Boaz's life. "'The Lord bless him!' Naomi said to her daughter-in-law. 'He has not stopped showing his kindness to the living and the dead.' She added, 'That man is our close relative; he is one of our guardian-redeemers.'" (Ruth 2:20) (Another, more familiar translation is "kinsman-redeemer.")

This last statement may have been as unfamiliar to Ruth as it is to some of us. Thanks to her time as a member of Naomi's family, and to her time in Bethlehem, Ruth was probably familiar with the basics of the Jewish culture. However, the intricacies of it would likely have still been unfamiliar. The laws and traditions probably had not made their way into Ruth's heart and mind. Thankfully, the same was not true for Naomi. We will learn more about the kinsman-redeemer process – another example of *hesed* – as Ruth's story unfolds. We also sense a new confidence beginning to grow in Naomi as she saw that God had more than a life of bitterness planned for her.

Ruth continued to talk, telling Naomi that Boaz extended an invitation to her to return to his field and glean during the remainder of the barley harvest. This was welcome news. "It will be good for you, my daughter, to go with the women who work for him, because in someone else's field you might be harmed." (Ruth 2:22) For the second time, we are alerted to the fact that the fields held potential danger for women. The fields could have been especially dangerous for Ruth, a Moabite woman with no male family members at home. She could easily have been mistreated, suffering anything from physical and sexual to mental and emotional abuse.

For the rest of the barley harvest, Ruth woke up each morning, left Naomi's home, walked to Boaz's field, and gleaned with the women. As far as we know, life was steady and stable. Naomi and Ruth's physical needs were met. Maybe Ruth felt like that was as good as it would get. If so, there were big surprises ahead of her.

Life-giver

In this portion of Scripture, we see three ways that Boaz provided for Ruth. Boaz invited Ruth to sit at his table and eat. Boaz provided an ample supply of food. Boaz blessed the life of Naomi through his interaction with Ruth.

Ruth was able to become a life-giver because of her relationship with Boaz. Boaz extended life-giving resources to Ruth, and she chose to receive them. Ruth sat at the table. Ruth gathered an ample supply of food. Ruth returned home to share her leftover provisions with Naomi. As a result, the lives of Ruth and Naomi were impacted and sustained.

As we walk with God during our time on this earth, He offers us the opportunity to be a life-giver like Ruth. We too have the chance to be impacted by Jesus and then to impact the lives of others. For a moment, think about this part of Ruth's story from a different perspective; this will help you to understand how you can be a life-giver too. Think of Boaz as the redeemer. (In many ways, the actions of Boaz foreshadowed the work of Jesus – the ultimate Life-source!) Think of Ruth as yourself. (We all need redemption!) Think of Naomi as the people God places in your life who need His love and grace. (You can fill in their names here!)

Daily we are invited to sit at the table with Jesus. As we sit, our lives are impacted. We leave the table, taking all that we learned with us, and live in a way that brings glory to God. As a result, the people around us are impacted by God's love and grace.

As we see the story of Ruth unfold, we are reminded of incredible truths. *It's not through our initiative that we come to God; He invites us to sit at the table.* We come to the table first and foremost *for ourselves*, not for anyone else. Once we leave the table, *we minister to others out of the overflow of what we have received.* Sometimes we think that we come to the table so we can fix our husbands, our kids, and our friends or colleagues. The point of coming to the table is much different– it's so that the Life-source can transform us. Boaz initiated the invitation, Ruth accepted, and, as a result, Naomi was provided for. God initiates, we accept, and our lives and the lives of others are changed.

To put it in other words, as women, we are influencers. We influence our husbands, children, friends, extended family members, fellow church members, and co-workers just to name a few. When we take time to sit at the table with Jesus, our lives are filled with His thoughts and clear direction. At the table, God changes us. We then have the chance to influence others in the right way.

The Call to Remain

A life-giver always takes time to interact with the Life-source. For believers, this means that we must daily interact with Jesus and walk with Him in a genuine way. A genuine walk with God is much different than a "check-list" kind of walk with God. In a "check-list" walk with God we may have a quiet time in the morning but then get lost in impatience or complaining throughout the day. In a "check-list" walk with God, we may send up a quick prayer but then fail to take time to listen for God's reply. In a "check-list" walk with God, we may go to church on Sunday but then forget about Jesus on Monday.

A genuine walk with God begins when we understand that each day we have an open invitation to sit at the table with Jesus. The invitation is always there, but there are many different ways to "sit at the table." We will explore some of them in the **Our Journey** portion of this chapter.

The gospel of John talks about staying constantly connected to Jesus and defines this process as *abiding* or *remaining*. Jesus said, "I am the vine; you are the branches. If you remain in me and I in you, you will bear much fruit; apart from me you can do nothing." (John 15:5) To *remain* in Christ means to dwell in Him.[xvi] If we long to live a life that brings glory to God and produces spiritual fruit that lasts, we will embrace the daily call to remain in Christ. In order to remain, there has to be a determination to connect with Jesus throughout our day even when surrounded by distractions.

If we are going to remain in Christ, we have to learn how to dwell in Him. We can relate the concept of dwelling to our homes. Our homes provide a place where we can let our guard down and be ourselves. In our homes, we can rest, renew, relax, and revive.

Our relationship with Christ provides the same opportunity. When we dwell in Him, we let our guard down and find a place where we can rest, renew, relax, and revive. Psalm 91:1-2 states: "Whoever dwells in the shelter of the Most High will rest in the shadow of the Almighty. I will say of the Lord, He is my refuge and my fortress, my God, in whom I trust."

The word *dwell* in Psalm 91:1 can be translated in three ways. Each of these meanings provides insight into how we can remain connected to Christ. First, *dwell* can mean a lengthy residence. Second, *dwell* can mean a short period of waiting. Third, *dwell* can mean a temporary visit.[xvii] Let's think about how we can relate these definitions to our dwelling process with Christ.

Sometimes we need to sit at the table with Jesus for a lengthy period of time. Maybe our hearts are overwhelmed because of a difficult circumstance, and these extended periods of time help us to focus on God and His sufficiency. I can think of one of the first times I had to embrace this type of dwelling in my life. I was a young wife and mother when the Lord called me to serve Him in full-time ministry. As busy as I was, and as inadequate as I felt, I knew I needed to enroll in seminary for more training. In the months leading up to seminary, I spent hours in God's Word. Every spare moment, I retreated to my bedroom and opened my Bible. I needed God's Word to speak to me in a real way. I learned to dwell with God with great intensity and focus for that specific period.

Sometimes when we are sitting at the table with Jesus, we are in a waiting period where we are "on hold" as we seek God's clear direction for life. In these periods, we need to dwell with the Lord as we wait on Him and His faithful timing in our lives. We need to avoid the tendency to try to figure out the direction of our lives on our own. We can remain connected to Jesus as we wait on Him to move on our behalf. For me, this may be the hardest part of the dwelling process. Simply sitting at the table and knowing that God is at work even when I cannot sense His movement requires faith. I remember a time when I had to use this type of dwelling process in my life. God gave my husband the idea of making a professional change. The waiting process itself seemed to take forever even though when I look back it was only a blip in eternity. Today, I am thankful for the lessons learned. Jay and I had to dig deep in our walk with God. Along the way, we built a closer connection with each other.

Most days, we simply need to sit at the table with Jesus through "temporary visits" that are made multiple times a day. Even if it's just for a minute or two, we can pause what we are doing and check in with the Lord. This daily practice allows us to stay connected to Jesus in a moment-by-moment way. When we check in with Jesus throughout our days, we invite Him (as well as the Holy Spirit) to help, teach, calm, redirect, and guide us. I learned the necessity of staying connected to Jesus like this several years ago. One night I was busy with all of my ministry "to do's." After hours of frustration and short tempers, the Lord asked me a life-changing question. He said, "Andrea, when you act like that, do you think your children know that I make a difference in your life?" Wow, talk about getting my attention! From that moment on, everything changed. Ministry for the sake of ministry was no longer worth it. Conformity to the image of Jesus—at work or at home—was my new goal. In order to be conformed to the image of Christ, I had to spend time with Christ, and I needed to do that multiple times a day.

Why should we want to remain or dwell in Christ? Remaining and dwelling leads to rest, renewal, and revival in our hearts. *In this way, our lives are increasingly filled with God's presence.* The outcome of remaining is the ability to bear God's fruit.

The Call to Produce

Daily we get the opportunity to display spiritual fruit as we walk with God. In fact, Scripture indicates that our lives will produce either spiritual fruit or self-centered acts. So the question is this: will we produce spiritual fruit that honors God and helps others? Or will we stay busy with self-centered actions that dishonor God and hurt others? If we want to produce spiritual fruit, we need to focus on the dwelling process. *The dwelling process directly impacts our ability to produce spiritual fruit.* We cannot produce something that is not cultivated in a consistent way in our walk with God. Spiritual fruit is the by-product of a spiritually focused walk with God.

Galatians 5:22, 23 identifies spiritual fruit. "But the fruit of the

Spirit is love, joy, peace, forbearance, kindness, goodness, faithfulness, gentleness and self-control." I wonder if these words are so familiar to you that you find it easy to read through the list, giving little thought to the power that it holds. If so, take just a moment to stop and think. Can you imagine walking through your day with a heart that is so saturated with Jesus that it touches everyone you interact with?

For example, what if each day you woke up and had an unexplainable amount of love for your husband and patience with your kids? What if you had an unexplainable peace about your job or studies, and self-control with your tongue and debit card? Can you imagine what it would be like to experience a joy-filled day even during a difficult season of life? What if you were able to show kindness to a person who has been less than kind to you? Through Jesus, all of the scenarios listed above are more than possible!

If we want to have spiritual fruit in our lives, we must remain connected to Jesus, our Vine. As we do, we will walk in step with the Spirit of God. We go where God tells us to go, and we do what God tells us to do.

Believers in Jesus Christ have an awesome privilege and responsibility to show the difference that Jesus makes in us. The very reality of our lives should be that others look at us and ask, "How can you have peace during this tragedy?" Or, "How can you be so patient with your kids?" Or, "How can you have so much joy every day?" We need to live the type of lives that provoke these questions. Each time these questions are asked, we need to be ready to answer it with a clear, "Only by Jesus' grace!"

When other people see Jesus in the way that we live, we're showing the qualities of a life-giver. I can't help but think of Ruth and her interaction with Boaz. Ruth was invited to be at his table and to feast on an abundant supply of food. Whether Ruth realized it or not, a personal relationship was forming with Boaz. The invitation provided the setting. The table provided the way. The food provided the nourishment. Ruth accepted all three. Naomi, who was not even aware that the meal was taking place, would benefit later from the encounter as well.

Our Journey

I get excited when I remember that when the Life-source impacts my life, the same Life-source can impact someone else's life through me! God works in many ways and often uses our lives to reach others. Daily we need to sit at the table with Jesus, take in an ample supply of spiritual food, and allow the spiritual food to make a difference in the way that we live. This is how God develops spiritual fruit in and through our lives.

In my own walk with God, I have discovered ten things that help me to consistently sit at the table with Jesus. These ten things were born out of the experience that I shared earlier in this chapter when Jesus asked me if my children saw the difference that He makes in my life. That moment changed everything. After that, I became intentional about sitting at the table with Jesus in meaningful ways.

1.   **Have a consistent quiet time.** *It is crucial for us to interact daily with God's Word.* Not only should we read the Bible, we should also allow it to impact the way we live. This means that the Bible should shape the way that we think, act, react, make decisions, and set priorities. Here are a few tips for a consistent Bible time:

- Pick a physical location that is free from distractions, pick a time of day that works best for you, pick a tool that you will use in addition to your Bible, and pick a pattern that will tell you how often you will have your quiet time.
- Have a plan and stick to your plan. If you are just beginning, use the 1-1-1 plan. Pick one book of the Bible, read one chapter a day, and claim one verse of Scripture. This plan makes reading the Bible "doable."
- Try to have your quiet time before the "reactive point" in your day. Your reactive point is the moment when you begin to react to the situations going on in your life. I've noticed that my own reactive point is when I turn on my computer or cell phone. From that moment on, I am reacting to life. When we have our quiet times before our reactive points, we are equipped to respond out of the overflow of God's Word instead of reacting out of our own nature. Having a consistent quiet time allows us to make spiritual progress in our walk with God.

2. **Memorize Scripture.** Obeying God's Word keeps us from making mistakes, and it provides a solid roadmap for us to follow. David proclaimed, "I have hidden your word in my heart that I might not sin against you." (Psalm 119:11) When God's Word is in our hearts, we have access to it 24/7. Throughout our day, we have choices to make; some of these choices require an immediate decision. When we have Bible verses memorized, the Spirit of God can bring a verse to mind that will guide us. The outcome of hiding God's Word in our hearts is an ability to make a wise decision that is based on truth. Here are some tips for memorizing Scripture:

- Pick a Bible verse, write it on a notecard, and carry it with you everywhere you go. Look for otherwise empty minutes in your day (waiting at the dentist, sitting in traffic, etc). and memorize your verse. Work on your verse a couple of minutes each day.
- Do not be afraid to memorize long passages of Scripture. By working through a few verses at a time, you can build your way up to having a whole chapter or two memorized. The Psalms are an easy place to start, and books such as Ephesians and Colossians are very applicable when it comes to dealing with everyday situations.
- When selecting a verse to memorize, pick a verse that speaks to an area of weakness or challenge in your life. For example, work on a verse on patience during family holidays, respect for those in authority during a crisis at work, or perseverance during exams. Choosing verses specific to your situation will help to fortify your faith journey.

3. **Journal your thoughts.** Recording God's work in our lives is too important to forget. I use journaling the most when I am struggling to understand a situation, and when I look back on it later I'm amazed at what God has done and taught me. I find that writing things down helps me to process deep emotions. As I write my thoughts, I recognize what is going on in my heart and can more easily turn my struggles over to the Lord. Here are some tips:

- Purchase a journal and begin to record God's work in your life. Decorate it, doodle in it—the more it feels like your own, the more you may want to write in it!

- Do not feel pressured to journal every day or for a certain length of time.
- If you are unsure how to get started, pick a Psalm from the Bible and make it your own. Rewrite the Psalm inserting your name and a situation that you face. This will help you to move head knowledge to heart knowledge as you claim God's Word.

4.   **Create a prayer closet.** I cannot overstate the benefit of a prayer closet. A prayer closet is a specific place to go when you need to be alone with the Lord. When my children were younger, I wanted to teach them to respect my time with the Lord. I also wanted them to see the connection between spending time with Jesus and the production of spiritual fruit. To do this, though, I had to get very practical by saying, "When I am in my prayer closet, you are not allowed to interrupt me unless it is an emergency." Here are some tips for creating and using your own prayer closet:
- Select a location in your home that is suitable. For example, my prayer closet is an actual closet in my room. It is a quiet place where I can go and shut the door in order to be alone. For others, their prayer closet may be a comfortable chair in the living room or a private spot on the back porch.
- Teach the members of your family to respect the important time that you spend with Jesus in this place.
- Go to the prayer closet often and spend a few minutes of uninterrupted time with Jesus. No cell phones or technology allowed!

5.   **Fill your life with godly friends.** It is important to surround yourself with people who love Jesus and encourage you in your daily walk with Jesus. Your close friends should hold firmly to the teachings in the Bible. Also, they should believe in you and want what is best for you. There is no place for competition or jealousy in these types of relationships. Godly friends tell you what you need to hear, and they express it in a way that lets you know that you are loved and valued, not only by them, but also by God. From time to time, it is helpful to take an inventory of your friendships.
- Determine if there are any friendships in your life that are a negative influence on you. If so, set new boundaries.

- Ask the Lord to bring friends into your life who are a positive influence on you. As women, we need to surround ourselves with godly people who cheer for us and challenge us in a Christ-honoring way.

6. **Have a balanced prayer life.** Following a prayer model helps us to have a balanced prayer life. Instead of just asking God for things, we can also learn how to praise God for the way He is at work in our lives and confess our sins. One simple method that I use is the ACTS prayer model.

A- Adoration: Praising God for who He is and the way He works.
C- Confession: Confess sins as well as where you are in your walk.
T- Thanksgiving: Give thanks for what God has done and is doing.
S- Supplication: Present requests to God for yourself and for others.

- Our prayers should be real and conversational. Any meaningful conversation has both talking and listening. It is easy for us to fixate on what we want God to do for us. When we focus on this, we miss all the ways that God is at work in our lives. It is therefore helpful to evaluate our prayer life and make sure that we are balanced.
- As you evaluate your prayer life, try writing out a few prayers following the ACTS model. Look for areas in your prayer life that are weak. Is it hard for you to praise God? Do you find that you shy away from confessing your sin? If so, work on your areas of weakness.
- Be sure to keep your prayer time real. When you connect with God honestly, you will find that your heart will change and grow. Prayer should feel like a heart to heart conversation with your best friend, not like leaving a message on a machine!
- Although a prayer model can be a huge help, avoid the tendency to become regimented in your prayer time. Remember, prayer is nothing more than an ongoing conversation with God. Keep it real, relational, and balanced!

7. **Embrace personal worship.** Personal worship is an ofter overlooked but beautiful part of a believer's walk with God. This can also be an example of dwelling in action. When I feel worried grumpy, sad, or mad, I try to take the time to worship the Lord. This

process allows me to take my eyes off of myself and put them on Jesus. Here are a few ways you can incorporate personal worship into your day.

- Use your iPod, radio, or CD player to listen to Christian music during your daily routines. This is an easy and fun way to focus on Jesus while you are doing laundry, cooking, cleaning, or exercising.
- Buy a hymnal or praise book and sing or read the lyrics to songs that remind you about God and His faithfulness.
- When driving in the car, choose to listen to music that enhances your focus on God.
- As you take walks, praise the Lord and think about all the things He has done for you.

8. **Choose to use good media in your life.** Whatever books, TV shows, magazines, or social media you enjoy, find ones that have a good influence on your life. We live in a day and age where we have access to so much media. This can be a temptation that inhibits our walk with God, or it can be a blessing that enriches it.

- Regularly evaluate everything that you read, watch, and subscribe to. Make sure that everything that you put into your heart and mind honors Jesus.
- Imagine you have a "Jesus filter" when it comes to media. Would you feel comfortable if Jesus was listening or reading or watching along with you?

9. **Fast from a "creature comfort."** Fasting is removing something so that we can focus on the Lord. We often associate fasting with food, but we can fast from anything that brings enjoyment or comfort into our lives. I find fasting to be helpful when I sense a special need to seek God's presence, overcome sin, or gain spiritual clarity. How can you fast in your life?

- Identify a "creature comfort" and remove it for a period of time. Your "creature comfort" might be coffee, chocolate, or a TV show. None of these is wrong any more than food is wrong, but removing one of them temporarily can give you a spiritual boost to focus on God instead.

- Before you begin your fast, determine the length of the fast and the purpose—this will make it more meaningful as well as keep you from giving up too soon.
- Start out with a short timeframe—a day, a week, or a month—and make sure that as you fast you focus on Jesus rather than on the item you are fasting from. While it is tempting, avoid filling your life with other things when you fast. Focus on Jesus and use your "hunger" to drive you to Jesus and His Word.

10. **Give it away.** When we give our resources away, we accomplish two things. First, we demonstrate the truth that every resource in our lives belongs to God. Second, we demonstrate faith that God will provide for our daily needs. Here are a few ways that you can give your things away.
- Instead of having a garage sale or taking part in a consignment event, ask the Lord to show you a person or family who needs the items that you have. Be open during this process, and watch God bring just the right person across your path. (Do not feel bad if you have a garage sale or pass along a good deal on clothes to a friend. The point of this exercise is to learn how to listen to God and His leading in your life).
- Take a certain amount of money and tuck it in your purse or wallet. Ask God to show you how He wants you to use that money for His glory.
- Use your time as a resource, especially if your funds are low. Try to set aside one hour a week and ask the Lord to show you how to use it to honor Him. This type of approach to giving makes a big difference in our walks with God. It teaches us to be sensitive to the way God is at work around us and to listen to Him throughout our days.
- When you sense a tug at your heart saying God wants you to give something away, respond in faith! Then watch God amaze you as He works in you and through you for His glory. It is an exciting process, so be ready and be open!

As you read through this list, do any of the ideas jump out to you? How can you put this idea into practice? Describe the link between remaining connected to Jesus throughout your day and the production of spiritual fruit. Give an example of how this has happened in your life, or how you would like to see it happen.

Conclusion

If just one of the ideas listed in the **Our Journey** portion of this chapter helps you to sit at the table with Jesus, do it! Do not be afraid to try new things when it comes to your walk with God. Be creative; know that you can and should use different approaches to remain connected to Jesus throughout your day. If we do the same things over and over again, we will find ourselves sliding into a spiritual slump.

A life-giver is a person who loves Jesus and longs for Jesus to fill their lives with clear direction and life-sustaining spiritual food. The result of sitting at the table with Jesus in a meaningful way is the production of spiritual fruit. When we are connected daily to the Life-source, life will flow through us to others!

In John 15:8 Jesus said, "This is to my Father's glory, that you bear much fruit, showing yourselves to be my disciples." Every day in our walk with God, we can bring glory to God and demonstrate to others that Jesus makes a difference in us. The key to this is daily remaining connected to Jesus, who is our Vine.

\

Chapter 6
Waiting and Watching

Her Journey

At some point after Ruth gleaned in the field of Boaz, Naomi had an idea. The idea was unselfish and shows us the affection that Naomi had for Ruth. "My daughter, I must find a home for you, where you will be well provided for." (Ruth 3:1) In contrast to the earlier chapters, we see Naomi centering her attention on Ruth. Naomi wanted Ruth to be taken care of and perhaps even loved.

In His goodness, God had made provision in the Jewish law and culture for people who were in situations of, "I am unlikely to succeed," "I fell on hard times," and "I have no one to care for me." The laws ensured that any member of God's chosen people could receive a fresh start, fair treatment, and help during a difficult season of life. Throughout history, God's heart has always been tender toward people in need of grace. These Jewish laws are outlined in Deuteronomy 25 and Leviticus 25.

We've already learned about some of the Jewish laws during our journey. However, there is another law that changed the direction of Ruth's life. This law was known as the law of Levirate marriage and provided the basis for Naomi's plan to find a home for Ruth. (To learn about this law, read Deuteronomy 25:5-10). The law of Levirate marriage ensured that the name of a deceased man would not be wiped out of Jewish culture if he died prior to having a son. If this happened, the dead man's nearest male relative was expected to marry the widow and provide a son who would carry on the name and inherit the land of the dead man.

The relative did not have to fulfill the Levirate marriage commitment although there was shame upon anyone who chose not to

Several benefits resulted from the Levirate marriage process. The name of the dead man was preserved, and the land remained in the family. It also ensured that a close family member would care for the widow of the dead man.

In the last chapter of this book, we saw how Naomi mentioned the term kinsman-redeemer (Ruth 2:20). Like the law of Levirate marriage, the kinsman-redeemer process was designed to help a family member during their time of need. This process included instructions for many different types of needs such as land issues, slavery issues, and trustee issues. It also gave guidance for avenging of a family death or providing an heir to carry on the family's name. The person who came to the aid of their family member in order to rescue them was referred to as a *goel*. This can be translated as "redeemer" or as "kinsman-redeemer."

There were three requirements that the kinsman-redeemer had to meet. First, the man had to be the closest living relative. Second, the man had to possess the necessary financial resources. Third, the man had to be willing to carry out the redemption process.[xviii] I find it fascinating how the kinsman-redeemer process foreshadowed what Jesus would do in coming to earth and dying on the cross. Only Jesus met the requirements to redeem our lives. Jesus took on flesh in order to become like us. Jesus lived a perfect life. Jesus went to the cross and died a cruel death so that we can truly live.

Naomi knew that Boaz was a close relative, close enough to be a kinsman-redeemer. At some point, Naomi had a daring idea—one that represented an epic turning point in her life. If you will remember, when Naomi and Ruth talked on the road between Moab and Bethlehem, Naomi believed that there was no hope for Ruth in Bethlehem. According to Naomi, there would be no husband, no children, and no hope for a meaningful future.

At this point in the story, though, we sense a much different tone to her words. Naomi was thinking clearly, formulating a plan, and instructing Ruth on the necessary steps. The transformation in Naomi's life was tangible; she was no longer living like a victim.

Naomi told Ruth, "Now Boaz, with whose women you have worked, is a relative of ours. Tonight he will be winnowing barley on the threshing floor. Wash, put on perfume, and get dressed in your best clothes. Then go down to the threshing floor, but don't let him know you are there until he has finished eating and drinking. When he lies down, note the place where he is lying. Then go and uncover his feet and lie down. He will tell you what to do." (Ruth 3:2-4)

Naomi was encouraging Ruth to place herself in a position where she would be accepted or rejected. There would be no middle ground. Ruth listened to Naomi and answered, "I will do whatever you say." (Ruth 3:5) I wish we could go back in time and watch Ruth walk to the threshing floor. Maybe she thought about her former life in Moab with Mahlon. I wonder if she remembered how Mahlon had courted her and proposed marriage. I wonder if she thought about the tears that she had shed since his death. As Ruth made her way there, going over every detail Naomi told her, I wonder if she thought, "Am I ready for this again?"

Once at the threshing floor, Ruth approached Boaz unnoticed. She lay down at his feet and waited. During the night, he was startled to wake up and notice a woman at his feet. Boaz asked, "Who are you?" (Ruth 3:9) Ruth revealed her identity, saying, "I am your servant Ruth." (Ruth 3:9)

Do not let the word *servant* fool you. It can also be translated "handmaiden" or "maidservant." Ruth was not relating to Boaz as an anonymous servant or slave who worked in his field. With this introduction, Ruth set the stage for her bold request. Ruth said, "Spread the corner of your garment over me, since you are a guardian-redeemer of our family." (Ruth 3:9)

The word *garment* that is used in verse nine can also be translated "wing." In the Old Testament, refuge, provision, safety, and shelter were found under the wing of God. Remember that Boaz praised Ruth in chapter two for her willingness to find refuge under the wing of God. In chapter three, we see Ruth seeking similar refuge under the wing of Boaz.

When Ruth asked Boaz to spread the corner of his garment over her, she was essentially asking Boaz to marry her! Once the request was made, there was no turning back. Ruth put herself and her future on the line. I imagine that one question resounded in Ruth's heart: "How will Boaz respond?"

"The Lord bless you, my daughter," he replied. "This kindness is greater than that which you showed earlier: You have not run after the younger men, whether rich or poor." (Ruth 3:10) Do not miss that Boaz used the word *kindness* or *hesed* to describe Ruth's actions. This time, however, the *hesed* was coming from Ruth to Boaz. The beautiful thing is that when we receive *hesed*, we are able to extend it to others. God showed *hesed* to His people throughout the history of Israel as well as when He sent Jesus to die on the cross. Throughout God's story, His loyal love has always been on display.

I can picture Ruth letting out a huge sigh of relief when Boaz affirmed her bold move. Boaz continued, "And now, my daughter, don't be afraid. I will do for you all you ask. All the people of my town know that you are a woman of noble character." (Ruth 3:11) Boaz did not applaud Ruth for her beautiful appearance (although Naomi had told her to wash, put on perfume, and wear her best clothes). On the other hand, Boaz did not discourage Ruth because of her questionable Moabite lineage. Instead, Boaz recognized the beauty of her heart. It blesses my heart that in the midst of a culture where women were treated as property or as a means to produce children, God raised up a man who treated a woman with honor and respect.

This exchange between Boaz and Ruth set in motion the Levirate marriage process. Boaz, a man of honor, next told Ruth that he was not the closest kinsman-redeemer. A closer relative existed and that relative had to be given the opportunity to redeem her first. However, Boaz did not allow this to stand in the way of blessing Ruth. Ruth spent the night at Boaz's feet and returned home the next morning with a shawl full of barley—sixty pounds of it, to be exact!

This barley was a gift from Boaz to Naomi; it confirmed to her both that Ruth had been to the threshing floor and that Boaz was serious abut the redemption process. Ruth told Naomi, "He gave me these six measures of barley, saying, 'Don't go back to your mother-in-law empty-handed.'" (Ruth 3:17) The barley also provided a gentle reminder. Naomi, who once viewed her life as empty, now had the opportunity to experience the abundance of the Lord. God was filling Naomi's life once again.

When Naomi asked about what happened at the threshing floor, I can only imagine the excitement and questions. Afterwards, Naomi instructed Ruth to wait and see what would happen. "Wait, my daughter, until you find out what happens. For the man will not rest until the matter is settled today." (Ruth 3:18)

Two very different lives lay before Ruth. A life bound to a stranger (the unnamed closer relative) or a life bound to Boaz, a man that she knew, trusted, and perhaps even loved. The last time that Ruth was at a crossroads like this, she was standing on the road between

Moab and Bethlehem. Think back to that moment. Even though that crossroads was hard and life changing, *Ruth was able to make that decision for herself.* She could choose between life in Bethlehem and life in Moab. At this point in Ruth's story, the circumstances were vastly different. Ruth had no control over the outcome of the kinsmen-redeemer process. She did not know who would redeem her life and marry her. All Ruth could do was wait and watch.

Waiting and Watching

Facing a crossroad in life can be daunting. While some are exciting, other crossroads are stressful since the outcome is unknown or beyond our control. These crossroads can show up in every area of life, beginning with birth and childhood and extending to relationships and parenting. They appear in our churches, our jobs, our finances, and our health.

We have all been there; we know what it feels like when a decision that will shape our future is in the hands of others. My life started with this type of crossroad. Before birth, I was put up for adoption. Several families considered taking me into their home, which meant my life could have gone in several different directions. I think about the different families that, for whatever reason, could not care for me. I think about my life and how it could have gone in several different directions. As a result, I can relate to this portion of Ruth's story. Like Ruth, I had to wait and watch in order to see which family God chose for me.

Waiting and watching are hard, but do you know what I have learned? While we're waiting and watching, our circumstances aren't in control. God is! God frustrates the plans that need to be frustrated, and He blesses the plans that need to be blessed. It wasn't until seven days after my birth that my adoptive dad and mom picked me up from the hospital and took me home. I finally had a home and a family, and it was the home and family that God chose for me. If you want to know why I am passionate about the waiting and watching process, it is because I know the value it holds. *Through the waiting and watching process we discover the journey God has for us.*

As humans, we wonder if God sees, cares, and remembers us during our time of need. However, as we learn to wait and watch, we learn to embrace God's timing and direction for our lives. My personal journey has been long and at times difficult. I will be honest and admi that sometimes I have viewed the first portion of my life as out of control. Today I know that my life was never out of control! God directed each event; in perfect faithfulness He took good care of me.

Jesus highlighted the importance of waiting and watching when He told a parable to His disciples. This parable dealt with Jesus' second coming and how His followers need to be ready. Jesus said, "Be dressed ready for service and keep your lamps burning, like servants **waiting** for their master to return from a wedding banquet, so that when he comes and knocks they can immediately open the door for him. It will be good for those servants whose master finds them **watching** when he comes. Truly I tell you, he will dress himself to serve, will have them recline at the table and will come and wait on them. It will be good for those servants whose master finds them **ready**, even if he comes in the middle of the night or toward daybreak. But understand this: If the owner of the house had known at what hour the thief was coming, he would not have let his house be broken into. You also must be ready, because the Son of Man will come at an hour when you do not expect him." (Luke 12:35-40, emphasis added)

Perhaps it is easy to see the relevance of this parable to Jesus' second coming. As believers, we know that we should wait and watch with hopeful expectation for Jesus' return. However, it may be difficult to understand the relevance of this parable to our daily crossroads. Crossroads like "Will I get the job?" "Will we finally conceive a baby?" or "Will the wayward child come home?"

Embracing the instructions to be ready allows us to see Jesus' work in our everyday life. When we are eager for Jesus' return, we live a life of faith that is certain and hopeful even during the uncertain seasons of life. We also live a life of longing for eternity. This longing helps us to put our current situation into an eternal perspective so that when we wake up each morning, we can look forward to what the Lord has in store for us throughout the day. When it comes to our daily crossroads, we can embrace a life of waiting and watching by following three steps.

The first step is this: **Be ready for Jesus to move**. Just like we should be ready for Jesus' return, we need to be ready for Jesus to move in the midst of our daily experiences. When we are ready, we are hopeful and excited about God's plan. It may not happen today, or even tomorrow, but at some point we will experience God's resolution to our situations. When we know that God is moving in the uncertain areas, it changes the way that we live. We wait and watch with God's power at work in us. This helps us to engage in life even when we do not know God's specific plan for some area in our lives. Do you remember Naomi's instructions to Ruth? "Wait, my daughter…" (Ruth 3:18) The instruction implied an active, not passive, trusting. Ruth was not instructed to "check out" during the waiting process but rather to "check in" and to trust that a resolution was on the way. The same is true for us. We need to be ready for God to move by knowing that His resolution is on the way. As a result, we do not give up when times get hard. Rather, we get involved in living the life God calls us to live with passion and purpose.

The second step is this: **Be convinced that the outcome is clear in God's heart and mind**. Think about this: God is the only one who knows the timing of Jesus' return to this earth. Scripture states that not even Jesus knows the day or the hour. Although the return of Christ affects every believer, the timing of His return is out of our control. Does this mean that our lives are out of control or that life is not worth living? Absolutely not! *God is the ultimate authority over our lives, He is directing the events of our lives, and He is fulfilling a plan in and through our lives.* God directs the events and uses humans to accomplish His purposes. In Proverbs we find an example of God's direction. "In the Lord's hand the king's heart is a stream of water that he channels toward all who please him." (Proverbs 21:1) God guides the hearts, hands, and minds of humans. Our lives are never out of control.

We see this truth beautifully displayed in the story of Ruth. Even though Ruth did not know which man would marry her, God did. At no point in Ruth's life was her future "up in the air." God had a plan, and He used Ruth, Naomi, Boaz, and an unnamed relative to fulfill this plan. What can we learn from this? We can know that God sees what is going on in our lives and is taking care of us in perfect faithfulness. (Important side note: sin – our own or that of others – has consequences. However, sin is not stronger than our God! Remember that God is a restoring God. He brings purpose to our pain and meaning out of our mess. If your life has been affected by the sin of others, know that God sees and willingly restores.)

The third step is this: **Be active through the waiting and watching process**. In Luke 12, Jesus said the servant in the parable needed to be focused on the task the Master gave him. In the same way we should be engaged in life as we wait and watch for God to move on our behalf. Times of waiting and watching should never be viewed as wasted. Instead, they offer an opportunity for spiritual growth and deep commitment to God and His will. As we wait and watch, every area of our lives is changed. Our hearts will be more in tune with God as we learn to identify the ways that God is at work in us and around us. As we identify these areas, we have the opportunity to join God. Joining God always leads to spiritual growth and helps us to walk in step with Him. Listen to the full instruction that Naomi gave Ruth. "Wait, my daughter, until you find out what happens." (Ruth 3:18) The words *find out* mean to perceive, understand, know, and discern.[xix] Naomi instructed Ruth to watch the events unfold and to know that in the end a clear direction would be made known to her. The bottom line of the waiting and watching process is this: *the journey is just as important as the outcome.* Through the journey we learn more about God as well as ourselves.

Why should we wait and watch when that is contrary to everything that we learn in today's world? Not to mention that waiting and watching are hard to do! In the midst of the call to wait on God and watch for His move, we have an incredible promise to claim. "Being confident of this, that he who began a good work in you will carry it on to completion until the day of Christ Jesus." (Philippians 1:6) What incredible news for us to hold on to during times of waiting and watching! God is doing a good work in our lives, and He is committed to the completion of that good work.

From the moment that we enter this world to the moment that we leave it, God is at work in us and around us. We do not have to wonder if God wants to complete His good work in us; He does. We do not have to worry that God has forgotten us in the process; He has not. We do not have to question God's level of commitment during our time on this earth; He is "all in" when it comes to you and me. The question is this: Are we "all in" when it comes to Him?

When we wait on God and watch for Him to move, we let go of the need to run our own lives. We deny the urge to over-plan, over-prepare, and over-organize our lives to the point where God is irrelevant. Instead we recognize that God is in the leadership position of our lives. We commit to follow His lead no matter how long it takes. When we wait and watch, we also avoid the tendency to manipulate the situation in order to reach our desired outcome. Instead,

81

we walk in step with His purpose for our lives. We can relax, knowing that God is able to direct our futures so much better than we can.

Our Journey

In a fast-paced world that values quick decisions and easy resolutions, how do we wait and watch? The answer is simple. *We just do it!* There are no short-cuts in the waiting and watching process. A life that values waiting and watching is a life that embraces a counter-culture approach to living.

Having an accountability partner is very helpful in the waiting and watching process. Naomi served as this type of person in Ruth's life. Once Ruth shared her situation, Naomi instructed her to wait and watch. When Ruth followed this advice, Naomi would be there to encourage her. If Ruth had refused to listen, Naomi could have asked questions to help Ruth refocus on the waiting and watching process. She could have challenged Ruth to examine her heart to see why she was pushing ahead of God or why she was attempting to manipulate the situation.

An accountability partner longs for us to live the abundant life that Jesus freely provides. This person loves Jesus, loves us, and willingly holds us accountable to Biblical principles. She asks tough questions and gives honest answers. Our accountability partner knows us well. She knows our strengths as well as our weaknesses. She is a person that we trust and can count on during any season of life. Often we try to navigate through life on our own but get sidetracked or lost along the way. An accountability partner helps us to stay on the right path.

It is important to note that the accountability relationship does not develop overnight. This type of relationship takes time to establish. It is also important to note that an accountability partner can come in the form of a like-minded friend or in the form of someone who is very different. We might be surprised by the partners that God selects for us! An accountability relationship is not necessarily built on common interests, similar life stages, or even paths that cross on a daily basis. An accountability relationship is a unique relationship that God places in our lives, like the one between a certain Moabite woman and an Israelite matriarch. Often we have to wait and watch for God to bring the right person across our path.

If you are in need of an accountability partner, ask God to provide one. Share your desire with the women in your church. Discovering this person will take time and effort on your part.

Once you start an accountability relationship, remember to keep it *focused* and *balanced*. You remain focused by making sure that the two of you take time regularly to ask the tough questions, pray together, and share how God is at work in your life. As a note, it can be easy to let go of the accountability portion of your relationship and just be good friends. This is not bad, as long as you remain accountable to someone else. Just know that the more you get to know your accountability partner, the more you will have to guard the accountability portion of your relationship.

If the two of you have agreed to serve as accountability partners for each other, keep the relationship balanced by making sure that one person does not dominate the interaction. Both people need to be encouraged through the accountability process. At times one person may have a greater need than the other person, which naturally happens in relationships. However, the one-sidedness should not become an ongoing pattern. If it does, step back, reevaluate the relationship, and make necessary changes in order to keep it reciprocal.

When it comes to waiting on God and watching for Him to move, an accountability partner can help you in the process. Simply knowing that you do not have to wait alone provides reassurance. As you wait and watch together, you can both share the joy that comes from seeing God at work in your lives. Also, you will both have the opportunity to grow in your faith as you challenge each other to live closer to the Lord. Through sharing the ups and downs of life and praying for and with each other, it's possible to build a strong bond that helps you both through the crossroads of life.

- What are some benefits of waiting on God and watching for Him to move?

- Have you experienced a time when you faced a crossroad in life and the outcome was beyond your control? How did you deal with it? Looking back, can you see a way God was working at that time?

- If you are currently facing a crossroad, think about the three steps that were presented in this chapter. Step one: Be ready. Step two: Be convinced. Step three: Be active. Which of the three steps helps you and why?

- Do you struggle with over-planning to the point where it becomes difficult for you to wait on God and watch for Him to move?
- How would an accountability partner help you embrace a life of waiting and watching? If you have an accountability partner, is the relationship focused and balanced? If not, what changes need to be made? If you do not have an accountability partner, what specific steps could you take in order to find one?

Conclusion

Waiting and watching are hard. It's tempting to look for a quick and easy resolution to our problems. Through the waiting and watching process, though, God reveals the desires of our hearts. If we are willing to wait and watch for God to move, then we are focused on His plan for our lives. If we are not willing to wait and watch for God, then we are focused on ourselves.

As Ruth waited and watched, God moved. We will soon see the resolution that God had planned for Ruth, a resolution that continues to change lives to this day.

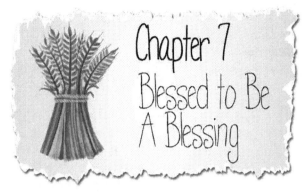

Chapter 7
Blessed to Be A Blessing

Her Journey

In Boaz's day, official business usually took place at the town gate. Unsurprisingly, Boaz selected this location as the place to discuss Ruth and her future. Boaz gathered ten elders to serve as witnesses, leaving no room for miscommunication, misperception, or mistakes. As Boaz and the elders sat at the gate, they waited for the nearest kinsman-redeemer to appear.

Before long, the nearest kinsman-redeemer passed by the gate. Yet again, we see an example of God's sovereignty in the story of Ruth. Boaz invited the man to sit down. Notice that the man's name is never mentioned. It is almost as if the author is hinting to us that this person is not going to be a key character in the story.

Boaz presented the following information to him. "Naomi, who has come back from Moab, is selling the piece of land that belonged to our relative Elimelek. I thought I should bring the matter to your attention and suggest that you buy it in the presence of these seated here and in the presence of the elders of my people. If you will redeem it, do so. But if you will not, tell me, so I will know. For no one has the right to do it except you, and I am next in line." (Ruth 4:3-4)

The presentation had been made, and it seemed simple. Naomi was selling Elimelek's land. The response of the nearest relative was straightforward. "I will redeem it." (Ruth 4:4) With great style, Boaz added one additional detail that changed the course of the conversation. "On the day you buy the land from Naomi, you also acquire Ruth the Moabite, the dead man's widow, in order to maintain the name of the dead with his property." (Ruth 4:5)

I'm curious about how Boaz's voice sounded in that moment, as well as about the thoughts of the other man. I imagine that the conversation had the elders on the edge of their seats. This type of transaction was taken seriously in Jewish culture. A family's name and lineage were at stake.

It did not take long for the kinsman-redeemer to realize that Boaz was presenting an offer that would drastically change his household. Not only would land be added to his possession, a wife would also be added to his home. This wife would be different from every other member of his family. This wife would be from Moab, a place that few Jewish men dreamed of connecting with in such a personal way. Also, a son would need to be provided in order to carry on Mahlon's name. The land would eventually go back to the son and provide a continued legacy for Mahlon's family.

It's possible that Boaz thought back to his own family tree at this moment. His mother was Rahab, an "unlikely" woman from Jericho. Like Ruth, she was a foreigner who had come to follow the One True God. Boaz would have experienced first-hand what came with the introduction of a non-Jew into their community. Like his father, Boaz would be taking a risk by marrying outside of his culture. But that would depend on the answer of the kinsman-redeemer.

As he digested the implications of the transaction, the kinsman-redeemer went from certain to unwilling. We can understand why the man replied, "Then I cannot redeem it because I might endanger my own estate. You redeem it yourself. I cannot do it." (Ruth 4:6) Hearing this, Boaz was ready to formalize his decision to buy the land. This occurred through the exchange of a sandal, a unique way that land deals were finalized. When the deal was made, Boaz knew that he could be the one to rightfully redeem Ruth's life. Boaz proclaimed to the elders, "Today you are witnesses that I have bought from Naomi all the property of Elimelek, Kilion and Mahlon. I have also acquired Ruth the Moabite, Mahlon's widow, as my wife, in order to maintain the name of the dead with his property, so that his name will not disappear from among his family or from his hometown." (Ruth 4:9-10)

The elders agreed and spoke a blessing over the union of Boaz and Ruth. "May the Lord make the woman who is coming into your home like Rachel and Leah, who together built up the family of Israel May you have standing in Ephrathah and be famous in Bethlehem Through the offspring the Lord gives you by this young woman, may your family be like that of Perez, whom Tamar bore to Judah." (Ruth 4:11-12)

This blessing carried rich historical meaning in the Jewish culture. Rachel and Leah married Jacob, and the two sisters, along with their maidservants, bore twelve sons. These sons became the heads of the twelve tribes of Israel; the tribes came to provide social and political structure for the nation of Israel. Every Jew knew the role of Rachel and Leah in the development of God's chosen people. In Tamar's story, we see the law of Levirate marriage as well as the kinsman-redeemer process in action.

When the elders sitting with Boaz asked God to make Ruth fruitful like Leah, Rachel, and Tamar, the implication was significant. The elders were asking God to enable Ruth to conceive and give birth to a child. God honored the request made by the elders, and I feel that He was also honoring the lives of Boaz and Ruth. God enabled Ruth to conceive, and she gave birth to a son, Obed. The birth of her son must have been a relief to Ruth since she was childless during her ten-year marriage to Mahlon, Naomi's son.

The next blessing came from the women of Bethlehem. I hope you remember the scene when Naomi and Ruth arrived from Moab. Naomi proclaimed that her life was empty, essentially dismissing the sacrifice that Ruth made by joining her. I imagine the women of Bethlehem wondered why Naomi would bring a Moabite woman home with her, but we are not told how they reacted or what they said.

At the end of Ruth's story, we see a much different scene. The feelings of the women of Bethlehem were displayed openly. The women said to Naomi, "Praise be to the Lord, who this day has not left you without a guardian-redeemer. May he become famous throughout Israel! He will renew your life and sustain you in your old age. For your daughter-in-law, who loves you and who is better to you than seven sons, has given him birth." (Ruth 4:14-15) So much had changed for Ruth and Naomi; God's work in their lives was obvious.

Notice what the women of Bethlehem were communicating to Naomi through their celebration. First, God had filled Naomi's life once again. She was not alone and empty any more. Second, Ruth was seen as a blessing, not a curse. The women of Bethlehem said that Ruth was better to Naomi than seven sons, and while that may not mean much to us today, it would have to Naomi. In Jewish culture, seven represented perfection or completion. Added to that, sons were highly valued, and to have many children was considered a special sign of blessing from God. The message that the women gave to Naomi was strong; Ruth was a perfect daughter-in-law for her and completed Naomi's family in a special way. I can just picture Ruth glowing when she heard the powerful words proclaimed over her life as well as the life of her son Obed. *Despite all odds, God used an unlikely woman from the sinful land of Moab to play a special role in Naomi's life, in God's chosen people, and in God's unfolding story of redemption.*

Next we read, "...then Naomi took the child in her arms and cared for him." (Ruth 4:16) Naomi's arms were full once again. No one would take the place of Mahlon or Kilion. Their lives mattered, and their legacy was secure in the hearts and minds of everyone who loved them. However, it was time for life to move forward. After the long season of hardships, God richly blessed Naomi and Ruth. Good days were ahead, and there was still life to live. The story of Naomi and Ruth was far from over.

As Naomi and Ruth embraced the sweet baby boy, they embraced God's healing and restoration in their lives. This embrace did not dismiss the hard times, nor did it erase the meaningful moments that happened before this child's birth. Rather, this embrace allowed Ruth and Naomi to physically touch the goodness of God right in the middle of their joy and pain.

Obed represented a fresh start, a new beginning. He was important in his own right; he did not need to live in the shadow of Mahlon, Kilion, or anyone else. God created Obed for a purpose, and no one but Obed would fulfill that purpose.

In Obed we see a link between the Old and New Testament. We can find his name in the family tree that is listed at the end of the book of Ruth, as well as at the beginning of the gospel of Matthew. Obed was a key player in God's unfolding story of redemption. Obed, whose mother was a Gentile, was the father of Jesse. Jesse was the father of King David. Generations later, Jesus would be born through this all-important family line!

Ruth, a Moabite woman, found herself woven into God's family in a very special way. At times in Ruth's story, the circumstances made it look like all hope was gone. However, at no point was God's plan paused. He was at work each step of the way.

Resolution through Relationships

To me, the theme of this final chapter of the book of Ruth is resolution through relationships. We see how each person involved in the story of Ruth both experienced a meaningful moment in his or her own life and shared a meaningful moment in the life of another. Think about it. The elders witnessed the meeting between Boaz and the near kinsman-redeemer. Boaz redeemed the life of Ruth. The women of Bethlehem blessed the life of Naomi. Ruth gave Naomi a grandson to love. Naomi cared for the needs of Obed.

In our lives, we have the opportunity to recognize and meet the needs of others. This process requires us to be intentional in the way that we live. We have to purposefully slow down. Getting involved in the life of others requires time and resources. This involvement takes energy, both physically and emotionally, especially when a situation is difficult or messy. *The bottom line is this: when we are serious about our walk with God we will embrace opportunities to bless the lives of others.*

In 2 Corinthians 8:1-15, the Apostle Paul encouraged the believers in Corinth to live a generous life. This passage of Scripture contains wonderful instruction that is applicable to many areas of our lives. Not only does it talk about financial generosity, it also has to do with our willingness to bless the lives of others through the way that we live. This passage speaks to the heart of finding resolution through relationships. It is important to note that our actions should come from competitiveness or a desire to feel needed. Rather, getting involved in the lives of others should be done as an extension of the grace that Jesus Christ has given to us.

Paul used the Macedonian churches as models of giving. Paul stated, "In the midst of a very severe trial, their overflowing joy and their extreme poverty welled up in rich generosity." (2 Corinthians 8:2) I find it reassuring to know that *times of hardship and trial do not limit our ability to bless others*. We always have the opportunity to give, and we can give in many different ways. In the final chapter of Ruth, we saw a perfect demonstration of creative giving. The elders gave their time to Boaz. The women of Bethlehem gave words of encouragement to Naomi and Ruth. Boaz gave Ruth a place to belong. Ruth gave Naomi the opportunity to care for a baby. Naomi gave her abilities to care for Obed. Each action was unique and met a specific need in the life of another.

The formula for generous living is found in 2 Corinthians 8:5. "They [the Macedonians] gave themselves first of all to the Lord, and then by the will of God also to us." Any time that we focus on the Lord and devote our lives to Him, our day-in-and-day-out walk will be impacted. We will find ourselves right in the middle of God's call to bless the lives of others. Let's examine this verse and see how we can embrace generous living.

"They gave themselves first of all to the Lord…"

Have you ever wondered what it looks like to give yourself to Jesus? If we have placed our faith in Jesus Christ for forgiveness of sins, we understand the first important step. But what does it look like to give our lives to Jesus each day after that? 2 Corinthians 8:5 answers this all-important question. The word *Lord* that is used in verse five carries the meaning of ownership. When we give ownership of our lives to Jesus, we accept the truth that our time, resources, and talents belong to Him, not us.

Most Christians would say that they understand the concept of ownership as it relates to Jesus. With our heads, we understand that our time, resources, and talents are not our own. However, I wonder how many of us actually show this in our daily walk with God. The concept of ownership cuts to the heart of the generosity issue. If we stop to recognize the length and depth of God's love for us and the price Jesus paid for us to be in a relationship with Him, our hearts will be changed. We can respond to this change by asking Him to govern our thoughts, actions, and reactions. We will also have a desire within us to see other people experience the grace of Jesus in their daily lives.

"…and then by the will of God also to us."

Giving ownership of our lives to Jesus leads us to discover God's will for our lives. If we are honest, we will recognize our limitations. There are so many people who are hurting and in need of support. It is a daunting task, and it's unrealistic to believe that we can be all things to all people all the time. *We need to be aware of when and how God is calling us to meet the needs of others.*

Discerning God's will requires daily communication with the Lord. Good communication involves two components—talking and listening. When talking to God, we present our praises, confessions, questions, needs and struggles to Him. Pouring out our hearts to Jesus leads to a deep sense of peace and helps us to clear our mind of the surrounding busyness.

When we are in the daily habit of taking time to communicate with God, we find it easier to listen to Him. Of course, listening to God is not as simple as receiving a text message, a phone call, or a handwritten note! It is, however, crucial to listen if we want to know God's direction for our lives. Listening will help us know when to move and when to wait. In the context of blessing others, we can know that God willingly directs us based on His plan. In 2 Corinthians 8, we see that the Macedonians were able to know the will of God on their level of involvement in the life and ministry of Paul. The same can be true in our walk with God as we give ownership of our lives to Jesus.

Sometimes we make discerning God's will harder than necessary. We can overthink things to the point that we are afraid to move forward in our faith journey. We can also run ahead of the Lord by giving little thought to His plans for our lives. So how do we know God's will in recognizing and meeting the needs of others?

God speaks to us in three main ways. Because we have the Holy Spirit of God living inside of us, we can sense God's voice and respond in faith.

First and foremost, God speaks to us through His Word, the Bible. We've already discussed how the Bible helps us on our faith journey. Another point that needs to be made is that God will never call us to do something that goes against the teachings found in the Bible. God's Word is our standard of truth. We can turn to it for direction, knowing that it provides instruction and reveals our motives.

Second, God speaks to us through the circumstances of life. God uses everyday experiences to lead us. We each go through hardships and triumphs, and through victories and defeats. Through our experiences, we can learn how to be sensitive to the needs of others. Perhaps God has done a healing work in your life after you were in an abusive situation, and you're able to reach out to someone in the same situation. Maybe you have been through a health crisis and as a result are more sensitive to others facing a similar battle. One way that God brings healing and restoration to our lives is when a hardships in life becomes an avenue for ministry. This ministry can provide a way for a hurt to be healed, a regret to be resolved, or a pain to produce godly purpose.

Third, God uses the encouragement of others to help us know how to live a life of faith. Have you ever noticed that other people can see strengths in you that you cannot see in yourself? I love this about the

Body of Christ. When a group of believers (a church, a Bible study, or an outreach team) is walking closely with God, there is a sense of unity and trust that lets members speak into one another's lives. God uses the encouragement of others to challenge us to step out in faith even when we think the step is impossible to take.

Isn't it good to know that God willingly speaks to us and through us? As we give ownership of our lives to Jesus, He faithfully guides our steps when it comes to recognizing and meeting the needs of others. 2 Corinthians 8:13 concludes with this important point. Paul wrote, "Our desire is not that others might be relieved while you are hard pressed, but that there might be equality. At the present time your plenty will supply what they need, so that in turn their plenty will supply what you need."

What a beautiful summary of life! We are blessed by God, and, in turn, we can be a blessing to the people God places in our lives! Just like Ruth, Naomi, Boaz, and Obed, we can find resolution through relationships. This resolution comes first in our walk with God and results in meaningful moments with the people around us.

Our Journey

There are many ways to recognize and meet the needs of others. We can do this in tangible ways with our resources and time. We can also do this in less tangible ways through the words that we speak. Take note of the fact that all of the individuals in the last chapter of Ruth met the needs of others in both tangible and intangible ways.

When it comes to the tangible ways of blessing others, even the smallest act of kindness can make a large impact. Things like taking a meal, sending a card, helping care for a child, or packing a box in preparation for a move can bless others beyond our ability to measure.

Often, the hardest part is knowing how to help a person in their time of need. I have found that the best way to help is by asking specific questions. I try to avoid a generic question like, "What can I do to help?" Instead, I try to be specific. "Can I take your laundry home and wash it?" "Can I bring a meal on Tuesday night?" "Can I drive carpool for you this week?" Some people may already have a need in mind, but others may appreciate a more specific request. Whatever the need, try to meet it in a loving way that honors Christ, not with an attitude of pride or impatience.

The intangible ways are often overlooked but make just as much impact. Two intangible ways of blessing others are being present in someone's life and speaking words of encouragement.

When we choose to be present, it lets someone know that they are loved, valued, and supported. We can be present in many ways. We can send a text message during a hard time, drop by a person's home for a visit, or remember a person in prayer. All of these actions recognize and meet a need in a very specific way. Chances are that we can find a way to be present in someone's life even if we do not have an abundance of time or resources.

When we speak words of encouragement, we have the chance to bless the lives of others. The significance of a spoken blessing cannot be overstated. The Bible is full of wonderful examples of God's people blessing one another, and the book of Ruth in particular provides several examples.

Have you noticed that the words of others can leave a scar in your life? This grieves the heart of God, but it happens often, even between His children. I am sure that you can think of examples of words that have hurt you. My question is this: can you think of words that have helped you? If so, you know the significance of a spoken blessing. Maybe the words came in a card, email, text, phone conversation, or face-to-face; it doesn't matter. They made an impact because they were delivered with love and sincerity of heart.

In the Old Testament, we find a special blessing, "The Lord bless you and keep you; the Lord make his face shine upon you and be gracious to you; the Lord turn his face toward you and give you peace." (Numbers 6:24-26) This passage of Scripture, along with others, teaches the importance of using our words to help others, not hurt them.

The idea of using a spoken blessing is new to me. While I try to use kind words with others, I hadn't recognized the Biblical model of blessing others with my words until recently. This changed the way I relate to others, and my family now intentionally takes time to speak blessings to one another.

On special events like birthdays, anniversaries, or "send-offs" to camps or activities, we take time to encourage the family member who is being celebrated or sent off. This time of encouragement involves each family member sharing one or two things that they recognize and value about the individual. We then pray for the person and ask God to bless them in a special way. Also, written notes in backpacks or lunch sacks can remind our family members that we are praying for them throughout their day. As a wife and mother, I am thankful that my words can build up the most important people in my life.

I also intentionally look for opportunities to speak words of encouragement into the lives of my extended family members and friends. Again, special occasions like birthdays, job promotions, and important life events offer opportunities to bless the lives of others.

One practical way to bless someone is to create a "top ten" list where you record things that you love and value about the person. Another way to bless is to write a letter to them and chronicle your family or friendship journey. In the letter, take the time to highlight all the ways that God has used that person in your life. There is a good chance that you remember details of your relationship that the other person has forgotten or never knew were important to you. If you've been praying for them, remember to share that, too.

Recognizing and meeting the needs of others in tangible and intangible ways is part of a genuine walk with God. When we invest in the lives of others, this shows our willingness to move beyond our own wants and needs. Like the people in the Macedonian churches, we too should be described in this way, "They gave themselves first of all to the Lord and then by the will of God also to us."

As you think about your ability and willingness to bless others, consider these questions:

* What is the hardest aspect for you of recognizing and meeting the needs of others?
* Which of the three ways that God speaks to us—the Bible, circumstances of life, the encouragement of others—helps you the most?
* Share one or two specific ways that you have blessed others.
* Describe one area where the Lord is calling you to respond to the needs of others. How can responding to this need help you move forward in your walk with God?

Conclusion

Naomi, Ruth, Boaz, and Obed were deeply blessed when the people around them purposefully got involved in their lives. We do not know the rest of the story of this unlikely family, but we do know that God worked in their lives and used others to encourage them along the way. As you think about your life and your story, know that the same principle applies. No matter how traditional or nontraditional your family is, God is at work.

I do not know about you, but often I am surprised by the plan of God for my life. Whether it is an unexpected blessing or a friendship that I never saw coming, God is faithful and always provides exactly what we need. It helps me to think of it this way: *the goal of life is resolution through relationships*. God sent His Son, Jesus, who died on the cross to save us. We have the opportunity to live our lives for Him and to bless others along the way—often in unexpected ways! Ruth, an unlikely woman from Moab, became a blessing to Naomi and to Boaz through her actions and through the birth of her son Obed. Hundreds of years later, another "unlikely" woman would be chosen to have a baby boy in Bethlehem. Her name was Mary. And her little boy would grow up to be the biggest blessing ever born.

I wonder how Ruth felt as she neared the end of her life. Did she look back on her extraordinary life and shake her head in surprise at how God used her in His plan? As you are on the road with God, know that He is calling you to a life that is bigger than yourself. He will provide all that you need and fill your life in extraordinary ways! Wherever you live and whatever crossroads you face, remember that God wants to bless you so you can be a blessing to others.

Epilogue

A long time ago, a woman named Ruth stood on the road between Moab and Bethlehem and faced a crucial decision. Would she return to her familiar life that had been or would she cling to Naomi and embrace the life that could be? We know the outcome of the story, and it was beautiful!

Little did Ruth know that she was answering a much bigger question for us. "Can God use someone like me?" Ruth embodied how God calls people from unlikely backgrounds and ordinary beginnings to take part in His amazing story. Even though she was a foreigner from a pagan country, Ruth still played a pivotal role in God's plan of redemption. During unsettling times of change, she experienced God's presence.

I think about my life and how I am faced with the decision to let go of what has been so that I can embrace what can be. I will be the first to admit that the life of Ruth challenges me. Let's think back and recap our journey together. We've examined how to have the right set of beliefs, display Christ-like character, and embrace an eternal perspective in life. We've also learned from the lives of the main characters in the story of Ruth. Through Ruth's life we have been challenged to:

- Cling to the right things in life
- Live with determination
- Engage in life
- Find our safe place in God and with others

- Be a life-giver who ministers out of the overflow of our relationship with Jesus.
- Wait and watch for God to move in our life.
- Bless the lives of others.

How about you? Are you inspired by Ruth's journey? More importantly, are you challenged in your own journey with God? Are you ready to display passionate trust even when life does not make sense? *Like Naomi, Ruth, Boaz, and Obed, you were born to fulfill a unique purpose in God's unfolding story of redemption.* This purpose was in God's heart long before you were born. Amazingly, you do not have to do anything to earn God's purpose. God's love and His plan for you are gifts of His grace.

I would like to end our time together with a quote that beautifully sums up the life of Ruth as well as sets the stage for our lives. "When God steps in, the ordinary events of life take on extraordinary significance."[xx] God has stepped in. There is no such thing as ordinary any more. You were created for an extraordinary purpose. My sweet friend, keep on pressing forward in your faith journey with God. Do not give up! Do not shrink back! Press on with all your God-given might!

ABOUT THE AUTHOR

Andrea Lennon
Wife | Mother | Christian Speaker | Author | Friend

Andrea fills many different roles. She is an "on the go" kind of girl who loves Jesus and shares His message of hope with those that she meets. From washing ball uniforms to speaking at women's ministry events, Andrea embraces life and daily looks for opportunities to grow in her relationship with Jesus.

As the founder of True Vine Ministry, her passion is to encourage women to know the truth, live the truth, and share the truth. Through speaking and writing, Andrea enthusiastically shares the teachings found in the Bible and helps women to apply the Bible to the everyday aspects of life. (Like how to stop yelling at the kids and kicking the dog!)

Andrea is a 2004 graduate of Southwestern Baptist Theological Seminary. She has written and published *Reflecting His Glory: From Conformity to Transformation* and *Free To Thrive: 40 Power-packed Devotions for Women on the Go.* She has also released a teaching DVD that complements *Free To Thrive.*

Andrea and her husband Jay live in Conway, Arkansas with their two sons, Jake and Andrew. On the weekends you can find the Lennon family watching a ballgame, working on a school project, serving in their local church, or hiking on a beautiful trail. Andrea travels extensively and thanks God for the opportunities to meet women, hear their stories, and teach the Bible.

To learn more about Andrea and True Vine Ministry, visit her website at www.andrealennon.net.

Free To Thrive
40 Power Packed Devotions for Women on the Go!

In *Free To Thrive* author Andrea Lennon presents a clear biblical picture of freedom through 40 power-packed devotions. Each devotion invites you to know and experience God's freedom in every area of your life. Free to Thrive topics include:

- Embracing God's definition of freedom
- Viewing sin through the eyes of a holy God
- Heeding the words of Christ
- Basing your life on correct theology
- Fighting a constant fight
- Doing whatever the Lord asks you to do
- Passing the point of no return
- Longing for your real home

Reflecting His Glory
From Conformity To Transformation

Reflecting His Glory: From Conformity to Transformation explores Romans 12:2. This study provides a step-by-step approach for you if you long to:
- recognize conformity in your life
- understand the call to spiritual transformation
- establish a daily process for renewal
- view God's will from His holy perspective, not your own.

Join Andrea Lennon as she leads you to discover life-changing truths that teach you how to think like Jesus, act like Jesus, and ultimately reflect the glory of Jesus Christ. Come away from this study changed, living for God's glory and not your own.

BIBLIOGRAPHY

[i] Spiro Zodhiates, *The Key Word Study Bible* (Chattanooga, TN: AMG Publishers, 1996), # 2876, 1516.

[ii] Merriam-Webster's On-line Dictionary, "Determination," May 28, 2013.

[iii] Trent C. Butler, *Holman Bible Dictionary* (Nashville, TN: Holman Publishing, 1991), "Hope," 665.

[iv] Merriam-Webster's On-line Dictionary, "Despair," September 24, 2013.

[v] Zodhiates, *The Key Word Study Bible*, # 4444, 1663.

[vi] *Holman Bible Dictionary*, "Joy," 819.

[vii] Ibid. "Peace," 1086.

[viii] Merriam-Webster's On-line Dictionary, "Strife," October 2, 2013.

[ix] Zodhiates, *The Key Word Study Bible*, #1538, 1612.

[x] Merriam-Webster's On-line Dictionary, "weakness," October 3, 2013.

[xi] Sandra Glahn, *Premium Roast with Ruth,* (Colorado Springs, CO:, AMG Publishers, 2007), 75.

[xii] Ibid.

[xiii] Merriam-Webster's On-line Dictionary, "Authority," October 25, 2013.

[xiv] Zodhiates, *The Key Word Study Bible*, # 2879, 1517.

[xv] *Holman Bible Dictionary*, "Humility," 676.

[xvi] Zodhiates, *The Key Word Study Bible,* # 3531, 1650.

[xvii] Ibid. # 3782, 1522.

[xviii] Rosenthal, Marvin. (2015, January-February) A Woman Named Ruth, *Zion's Fire, Volume 26* (Issue 1), 12.

[xix] Zodhiates, *The Key Word Study Bible,* # 3359, 1520.

[xx] David Alexander, *Eerdman's Handbook of the* Bible (Carmel, New York: Lion Publishing, 1973), 228.

Made in the USA
Columbia, SC
22 March 2023